Losing Your Executive Director Without Losing Your Way

Carol Weisman
Richard I. Goldbaum

Losing Your Executive Director Without Losing Your Way

The Nonprofit's Guide to Executive Turnover

JOSSEY-BASS
A Wiley Imprint
www.josseybass.com

Published by Jossey-Bass
A Wiley Imprint
989 Market Street, San Francisco, CA 94103-1741   www.josseybass.com

Jossey-Bass books and products are available through most bookstores. To contact Jossey-Bass directly call our Customer Care Department within the U.S. at (800) 956-7739, outside the U.S. at (317) 572-3986 or fax (317) 572-4002.

Jossey-Bass also publishes its books in a variety of electronic formats. Some content that appears in print may not be available in electronic books.

The quotation from Sage and Burrello in Chapter Three (p. 27) is reprinted with permission from Sage, D., and Burrello, L. *Leadership in Educational Reform: An Administrator's Guide to the Changes in Special Education.* Baltimore, Md.: Paul H. Brookes Publishing Co., Inc., 1994.

The bulleted list from Price Pritchett in Chapter Three (p. 31) is reprinted with permission from Pritchett, P. *Culture Shift: The Employee Handbook for Changing Corporate Culture.* Dallas: Pritchett, LP, 1993.

The poem by Karl Albrecht in Chapter Three (p. 32) is reprinted by permission of Harpercollins Publishers from Albrecht, K. *The Only Thing That Matters: Bringing the Power of the Customer into the Center of Your Business.* New York: Harper Business, 1992.

The example describing The Delta Center Board decision-making process in Chapter Eight (p. 130) is reprinted with permission of The Delta Center for Independent Living, 5933 Highway 94 South, Suite 107, St. Charles, Missouri, 63304.

Library of Congress Cataloging-in-Publication Data

Weisman, Carol E.
   Losing your executive director without losing your way: the nonprofit's guide to executive turnover/Carol Weisman and Richard I. Goldbaum.—1st ed.
     p. cm.
   Includes bibliographical references and index.
   ISBN 0-7879-6371-2 (alk. paper)
    1. Nonprofit organizations—Management. 2. Chief executive officers—Recruiting. 3. Chief executive officers—Selection and appointment. I. Goldbaum, Richard I., date. II. Title.
   HD62.6.W46 2004
   658.4'0711—dc22

2003023379

Printed in the United States of America
FIRST EDITION
HB Printing   10 9 8 7 6 5 4 3 2 1

Contents

This book is dedicated to the memory of Dick's stepson,
John Adam Miller,
And Carol's mother-in-law,
Beatrice Noback Robbins.

Preface

The departing Executive Director (ED) meets with the incoming ED to ease the transition. As the departing ED is leaving, he hands the new ED three sealed envelopes and says: "As your work with this organization progresses, you will inevitably run into some rough times. I have numbered each envelope: 1, 2, and 3. Open the envelopes in sequence, one for each episode. I hope the advice in them will enhance your tenure with the organization."

Within the first six months a few minor rumbles begin and things are somewhat stressful. The new ED opens envelope 1 and reads: *"Time to blame the problem on your predecessor."* The new ED begins to imply the problem is related to what her predecessor left behind. The problem quickly resolves itself.

Four years pass and again the Board of Directors and staff are restless. One day the ED notices envelope 2 in her desk and quickly opens it to find this message: *"Time to reorganize."* The ED starts reorganizing the staff, administration, fundraising, and programs. The problem that was festering soon dissipates.

The ED is a few months from celebrating her tenth anniversary with the agency when the relationship with the Board begins to change significantly. It seems that when she says an issue is white, they perceive it as black. She sees many other indications that she is in deep trouble with the Board. One evening the ED is working late when she comes across the third envelope. She quickly remembers how helpful the two previous envelopes were, so she opens it and reads: *"Time to prepare three envelopes."*

Some nonprofits have to hire a new ED every few years, while others may go for decades without a change. An ED's departure is one of the most significant events that can occur in a nonprofit organization. How this departure is managed and how the next ED is hired and welcomed will determine the success of the organization for many years to come. Nonprofit organizations have enough challenges today that create instability and threaten their survival without having to fear the inevitable executive transition.

This book was written to assist nonprofit organizations with executive transition and inform them of the process and concept of transition management services (TMS): a compendium of activities that form the bridge between the organization's previous ED and the new one. Members of Boards of Directors, people currently serving as EDs, and private and public funding entities that invest in the nonprofit sector will find its contents helpful.

January 2004

Carol Weisman
St. Louis, Missouri
Richard I. Goldbaum
Chesterfield, Missouri

Acknowledgments

One or two people never write a book. It's always a group project. Special thanks to

- Dorothy Hearst, our wonderful editor at Jossey-Bass, who is unfortunately not related to the zillionaire Hearst family and so unlikely to buy any of our clients a building.

- Marilyn Dickey, who helped us reorganize chapters when we were too close to see the proverbial forest. She never made us cry or feel stupid.

- Dennis Fletcher, our cartoonist, who came up with ideas as well as fabulous drawings.

- Rose Jonas, a member of Carol's elite plus-size running group, the Chafing Dishes, who read the initial manuscript.

- Tim Wolfred, who reviewed this manuscript in its very, very early stages.

- Carol's mastermind group—Lois Creamer, Tony Ruesing, Steve Epner, Sam Silverstein, Linda Nash, and Karyn Buxman. Nothing happens without their help and support.

- Dick's former partner, Margaret "Maggie" Michael, was a significant contributor in the early development of the concept of executive transition and interim management in his company.

- Tom Adams, who also gave us input and encouragement in the early stages.

- Our agent, Jeff Herman, who negotiated the deal with Jossey-Bass that provided us with the first-class cabins on the *QE 2* for a month so that we could finish the book in style.

- And as always, to our spouses, Jo Ann Goldbaum and Frank Robbins, who always trusted us together. How depressing is that!

C.W. and R.I.G.

The Authors

CAROL WEISMAN is President of Board Builders Inc., which is committed to helping nonprofits achieve greater success and Board and staff members find greater joy in their work. Weisman is an internationally known speaker, author, and trainer, her popularity no doubt fueled by the fact that she is one of the few nonprofit experts on the speaking circuit who also does stand-up comedy.

Weisman is the author of six books on nonprofit management and fundraising and is featured in two Telly Award–winning videos: *Speaking of Money* by BoardSource and *Building a Board with a Passion for Mission* produced by the Learning Institute for Nonprofit Organizations and PBS. Weisman has her MSW from Washington University in St. Louis and her Certified Speaking Professional designation from the National Speakers Association.

She is the mother of two grown sons and has been married for twenty-seven years to her honey, Frank Robbins. When not speaking, writing, or consulting, she trains with an elite group of plus-size runners called "The Chafing Dishes."

RICHARD I. GOLDBAUM is the owner and principal of Transitions In Leadership, a St. Louis–based firm that provides services for planning and implementing leadership and organizational change for nonprofit organizations. These services include placement of interim

Executive Directors, conducting executive searches, and facilitating the strategic planning process. Goldbaum has more than forty years' experience working with nonprofit organizations; twenty-five of those years were as an Executive Director. He received his doctorate in 1972 from St. Louis University. He is the recipient of numerous awards in the field of developmental disabilities, and is a frequently requested speaker on leadership transition, nonprofit management, visioning and planning, and board-staff relationships. The unashamedly proud grandfather of Gabe, Mason, and Isaac, he lives in St. Louis with his wife Jo Ann and a fish named Jaws.

Losing Your Executive Director Without Losing Your Way

Introduction

The Seven Components of Successful Transition Management

Leadership in nonprofit organizations is shared between the volunteer Board members and a paid professional. The paid professional might be called the President, the Chief Executive Officer, the Director, Principal, Headmaster, Artistic Director, or any number of other terms depending on the mission and the history of the organization. For simplicity, this book uses *Executive Director* or *ED* to describe anyone in one of these jobs.

The Board represents the interests and values of the community, the members and consumer groups served by the organization. The ED represents the management, professional expertise, and values needed to ensure that the organization's operations are of the highest quality and efficiency possible. The Board determines what should be done; the ED is responsible for how it's done. The Board and ED have a shared responsibility for creating and working toward the organization's vision, mission, and core values.

As long as the ED fulfills the expectations of the Board and vice versa, both leadership entities will thrive. As with all good things, however, this relationship will eventually come to an end.

The ED's departure—which initiates executive transition—may be planned or abrupt, viewed with sadness or relief, well organized or chaotic. Whatever the circumstance, it is a challenge that all Boards of Directors will inevitably face—and many Boards face quite frequently. The average tenure of Executive Directors of non-profit agencies is three to seven years, according to a number of studies including the Stevens Group (1998), Neighborhood Reinvestment Corporation (1999), and CompassPoint (formerly the Support Center for Nonprofit Management; Wolfred, Allison, and Masaoka, 1999).

Despite their frequency, though, executive transitions are often problematic. An ED's departure is indeed stressful under any circumstances—but it can also be the impetus for positive change.

According to Frances Hesselbein, President and CEO of the Drucker Foundation for Nonprofit Management and former CEO of the Girl Scouts:

> Few events in the life of an organization are as critical, as visible, or as stressful as when the leader leaves the organization. The eyes of every employee, customer, partner, and investor are focused on the outgoing executive. How that moment is managed reveals the character and effectiveness of the leader, the organization, and its people. . . .
>
> Leadership transition is an integral process for all leaders of an organization. It begins before (and continues long after) the outgoing leader departs, and presents a remarkable opportunity to move forward with a new understanding of the complexities, challenges, and changes the organization must address [1997, p. 7].

This book will take you through seven steps that can help smooth the way from one leader to the next and help keep the organization afloat through the sometimes rough waters of Executive Director transitions:

1. *Preparation:* The first step happens long before the ED even considers stepping down. Every organization should prepare

itself for the time when its ED leaves. Preparing for the inevitable is a responsibility that rests with both the Board and the ED.

2. *Response:* The ED's departure can create a void in staff leadership that the Board must address immediately. Its actions must take into account the response of the staff, clients, funders, community, and other stakeholders. The Board must also step back and look at its own response as it begins the process of finding a new ED.

3. *Hiring an Interim ED:* If there will be a gap between the outgoing leader and the new ED, the Board may want to fill the position with an interim Executive Director. It may also want to consider doing so if the organization has serious problems and would benefit from having an objective, experienced professional institute some changes and clear the way for the new permanent leader.

4. *Recruitment and Screening:* The decision of how to conduct and structure the executive search process determines the amount of time, money, and skills needed by the Board.

5. *Negotiations and Hiring:* Offering the ED's position to the best candidate may be the most critical action a Board can take, and choices made during the negotiations of employment may determine the long-term relationship between the ED and Board.

6. *Orientation:* It is important that the new ED start off in the right direction with the Board, staff, participants in the organization's services, and other stakeholders. The ED's introduction to the organization and the community at large takes planning and coordination.

7. *Retention:* Holding on to the newly hired ED requires commitment, communication, and all the other skills of relationship building. The departing ED may be stepping down due

to problems that could have been avoided. Identifying those problems before the new Executive Director comes on board can help the organization avoid repeating that experience.

1

Why Executive Directors Leave

E xecutive Directors leave for a variety of reasons. Sometimes departure is on good terms, other times not. In this chapter, we explore why nonprofit leaders move on—and how to determine whether the time has come for a change of leadership.

Seven Key Factors

We have identified seven reasons EDs leave their jobs. There may be others, but we chose to limit ourselves to seven. Seven seemed like a good number. There are seven deadly sins. Covey found seven habits of highly effective people. Seven is a lucky number. There are seven dwarfs. There are seven days in the week. So we decided to stay with seven:

- The Career Ladder Factor
- The Godfather Factor
- The Gone Fishing Factor
- The Sudden Loss Factor
- The Burnout Factor
- The Cutting the Mustard Factor
- The Ten-Year Factor

THE LEVEL OF SENSITIVITY AMONG BOARD
MEMBERS TOWARD EXECUTIVE BURNOUT
VARIES GREATLY

If you look at any executive transition, you're likely to see that one of these seven can explain much of what's happening. The following sections describe how it works.

1. The Career Ladder Factor

Most self-improvement theories focus on the need to succeed and be recognized for our abilities. We all have the desire to improve ourselves and prosper and be upwardly mobile.

People enter the nonprofit world with expectations of doing good for others and the community. They usually make conscious decisions and accept realities that a position with a nonprofit organization will not lead to great wealth. Consider EDs who at the height of their career are spending fifty to sixty hours a week to position the organization to succeed but who get little or no financial reward for the sweat equity. One ED used to complain because his wife always criticized him for spending so much time at work and not enough with his family. She often reminded him that when he left he would not be able to sell the organization and take the profit.

Altruistic motivations soon run into the reality of needing to support a growing family, keeping up with the cost of living, and mundane realities such as replacing an aging car and not knowing where the payments will come from. It is usually at that point that EDs start to realize that altruism is not totally fulfilling their life's goals.

The desire to make a difference and the desire to maintain a decent style of living often come into conflict. And when the drive to succeed and prosper is too strong, most EDs keep their options open and respond to new professional opportunities with higher salaries.

2. The Godfather Factor

When an organization is fortunate enough to have a competent and successful ED, it may be subject to the envy of others that are less fortunate.

Competition for seasoned and proven leadership is a fact of being part of an industry in which competency is valued and highly sought after. Don't be too surprised when your ED tells your Board about receiving an offer that could not be refused.

The Board should be proud that it has an ED some other organization wanted. It's always good to be seen as having competent leadership. The challenge will be to find a replacement with similar talents. Who knows—you may be in the position to make a candidate for your ED's position an offer likewise impossible to refuse.

3. The Gone Fishing Factor

How many times have you thought how great it would be to retire? Based on recent census figures, the largest group in our society is the baby boomers, who are now nearing retirement age. It is safe to say that as the population is graying, so are the vast majority of EDs. Change in hair color may or may not be related to age, only your barber or hairdresser knows for sure. But many top executives are reaching that enviable period in their lives when they will be leaving their positions to pursue other interests: going fishing or playing golf or something else unrelated to their current work. In a recent study the United Way of New York City found that close to 50 percent of the Executive Directors surveyed were planning to retire within the next five years.

The retirement of an ED is often announced well in advance and thus provides the Board with an opportunity to take time and plan for the transition.

Ideally, the Board should always identify an heir apparent before the ED is ready to resign, but impending retirement makes it particularly opportune to do so. The ideal successor may already be employed by the organization, but if not, the Board will need to recruit one.

4. The Sudden Loss Factor

A Board we worked with was in a regularly scheduled meeting. Attending for the first time were three newly appointed Board members. As the meeting progressed the Board President asked if there was any new business. One new member raised her hand and asked: "What will we do if tonight, on his way home, our ED is hit by a Mack truck, injured, and out of work for six months—or even killed?" There was dead silence until someone spoke up and said the Board had not addressed such a scenario. The Board President, feeling awkward and wanting to avoid a morbid discussion, asked that the new member come to the next meeting with suggestions for addressing the scenarios she had raised.

It is not comfortable to discuss your own possible injury, illness, or demise, or that of a trusted and well-liked employee. But the Board must address the sudden loss of an ED. Most of us have known someone who was suddenly severely injured or killed in an accident, contracted a catastrophic illness, or unexpectedly died from a heart attack. The sudden loss of a leader naturally causes sadness, but it may also cause organizational immobility and crisis. Sadness will heal in time; immobility and crisis, however, may linger and fester if not addressed immediately.

Having a plan that gives specific directions for action is especially important at this time.

5. The Burnout Factor

The stress of working in the nonprofit arena is well known to most EDs. These are some of the many challenges associated with the role:

- Being responsible for meeting the organization's mission with limited and unreliable funding resources

- Keeping up with the details of human resource management

- Working with a volunteer Board with its various personalities and differing management styles and expectations

- Adjusting every few years to new Board leadership and changing expectations and priorities

- Complying with unfunded mandates from funding sources, such as keeping a separate set of books

- Competing for staff, volunteers, and fundraising resources

- Working long hours with low pay and a poor compensation package

- Growing pressure to be both fiscally and programmatically accountable

Job burnout is a common reason for ED's departing. Burnout alone may be the major reason many EDs (86 percent) leave for positions in the for-profit sector (Wolfred, Allison, and Masaoka, 1999). In Chapter Eight, we review strategies for Boards to consider on how to reduce ED stress and burnout.

6. The Cutting the Mustard Factor

There was a time when harvesting the mustard plant was difficult and hard work. It required skill and speed, and if you couldn't keep up and did not meet your quota you were fired. In today's highly competitive world, if an ED does not maintain the expected level of competency and productivity, the Board may initiate a change as briskly as any mustard farmer. Considering the pressures inherent with the job, some EDs have trouble satisfying all aspects of the job. Oftentimes an ED resists learning new skills or adapting to new technology.

In any case, not cutting the mustard is an unfortunate way EDs leave their position.

And even an ED who otherwise performs to expectations can succumb to the temptation of doing something that is illegal, immoral, or unethical. No employer should tolerate those behaviors, which could lead to terminating the ED "for cause."

Whatever the reason, the ED serves at the pleasure of the Board and may be fired at any time. Most EDs do not have contracts, and those who do are still required to maintain a high level of competency.

Bringing in the mustard harvest was hard work, and so is being an ED of a nonprofit organization. It requires skill, adaptability, accountability, and productivity. An ED who can't or won't cut the mustard may need to vacate the position.

7. The Ten-Year Factor

There is something mystical about approaching the tenth year as an organization's ED. We have seen too many good EDs leave their positions when their tenure reached a decade, give or take a couple of years. We have no scientific research to explain this phenomenon, only anecdotal records from our work in the field.

Many EDs find that as they approach their tenth anniversary with an agency, their relationship with the Board begins to change. The change may begin subtly, as the ED becomes too secure in the position. After ten years, those individuals who served on the Board when the ED was hired are usually no longer there (especially if the organization has term limits in the bylaws).

The present Board members may differ from those who hired the ED in many ways:

- Expectations for the conduct of the job

- Visions and concepts of the organization's mission

- Core values

- Service and program priorities

- Styles of governance

The ED may begin receiving subtle signals that the once-supportive and trusting relationship with the Board has changed.

The ED who stays around for ten years may also have changed—becoming stagnant, worn out, and demotivated. The enthusiasm, dedication, and physical and mental energies the ED once brought to the job may be waning. A change can offer new challenges, new opportunities, and a new environment in which the ED's skills may be just what are needed. This may be just the right time to prepare those three envelopes.

Spotting Trouble and Damage Control

A Board has a number of options for avoiding executive transition in the first place. The Board should anticipate why EDs may consider leaving for those factors that are within their control (the Career Ladder and Godfather Factors).

Pay Attention

Research says that most staff members who leave their jobs rarely do so because of money. This may be true generally speaking, but if EDs are at a certain point in their career, they may leave because they are ready for a position with more challenges, more security, and better compensation—especially better benefits, such as retirement, medical-dental-vision insurance, and an agency vehicle. The Career Ladder and Godfather Factors may be in play as well when EDs leave in search of improved compensation.

The Board is responsible for ensuring that the ED's compensation package is competitive with offerings from similar organizations within the community. It is useful to review the compensation package provided all employees—including the ED—at least every three to five years. This process will keep the Board informed as to where the organization stands in terms of being able to recruit and retain good staff.

Knowing the marketplace and keeping up with the competition will also prevent the phenomenon often called "sticker shock." Boards may have an unpleasant surprise when the ED leaves and they start the recruitment process. Most organizations face the problem of raising the ED's compensation package to a competitive level all at once rather than doing it gradually over the years. There are many tools to help Boards stay current. Executive salaries are available on www.guidestar.com, in the nonprofits' income tax forms—their IRS Form 990 filings—which contain the top five staff salaries for each reporting organization. Another place to find salary information is the yearly postings in industry newspapers, such as the *Nonprofit Times* (www.nptimes.com) and the *Chronicle of Philanthropy* (www.philanthropy.com).

Include Some Maneuvering Room

Include in the benefit package an opportunity for the new ED to take a sabbatical for three to six months after being with the organization for seven or more years. Sabbatical leaves are a new concept in the nonprofit world, but they have been used extensively in academia. The concept of leave with pay for more than a few weeks to do anything the individual wants may sound radical and inefficient, opening the Board to criticism. But a sabbatical may be just the thing to revive a tired and nearly burned-out ED. It also may give the organization an opportunity to test the leadership skills of members of the management team, who will be called upon to carry on the daily operations of the organization.

Many EDs decide to leave long before the working relationship with the Board has deteriorated. They know their leadership skills have brought the organization to its present position but realize that someone with different skills and expertise is now needed and it's time to let a new ED guide the organization to the next level. Knowing when to leave under these circumstances is a true sign of leadership, showing that such EDs are people who understand their own strengths and limitations, and what is best for their organization as well as their own careers.

But EDs are not always so insightful. Some of the trickiest decisions come when things haven't been going smoothly: The ED isn't right for the job, there's a growing rift between the ED and the Board, or, worse, a public scandal has erupted. Even the best organizations occasionally find themselves in the awkward position of having to decide whether to terminate the relationship or try to work things out. It's a critical juncture and both the Executive Director and the Board must carefully weigh their options. As the classic country western song goes, both the Board and the ED need to "know when to hold 'em and know when to fold 'em." We have seen too many Boards and EDs who were slow to address the problem because they were in denial or preferred to avoid an unpleasant situation.

Boards that believe the ED isn't cutting the mustard have to go through a similar decision-making process. Many try to work with the ED, providing mentoring, a management coach, or other supports to improve the ED's skills, or they offer attendance at a management or leadership training program. These measures may be based on a genuine hope that things will work out, or they might be simply an attempt to avoid the challenges of executive transition. Nevertheless, taking these steps is often commendable and may result in successfully changing the ED's performance, and thus improving the Board's level of confidence.

But if the ED's performance remains sub par despite all efforts, the Board must act quickly and decisively. If not, staff morale may deteriorate, the quality of programs and services may decline, and funding sources may begin to lose confidence. Most important, those who rely on the agency for services may suffer. Board members should step back and try to be objective. For example, Board members who work in the for-profit world should use their own businesses as a model and ask themselves, "Would I tolerate this in my company?"

We have seen too many Boards avoid making the tough decision until something occurs that leaves no other choice but to take action. That something may be an exposé in the local news media, a major funder's decision to bring the issue to a head, or staff members' taking action and seeking the Board's attention. How Board members get the wake-up call may or may not be important. The critical issue is that they get it and respond to it quickly and appropriately.

If the termination of an ED has the agreement of the full Board, the decision is uncomplicated. But if the Board is not in total agreement, it should hold a meeting where open and candid conversations are encouraged, where all sides are provided opportunities to express their opinions. Allowing all factions the chance to express their positions is important. Unilateral decisions will cause irreparable harm to the Board. Employing an independent consultant as a facilitator to the Board's deliberations can be useful when the board is faced with differing opinions, as the objectivity of a skilled facilitator can help the Board reach consensus and come away with a decision that everyone will support.

The ED's Side of the Question

In general, once the Board has reached its decision to terminate the ED, it is not appropriate for the ED to attempt to generate or manipulate support from Board members. We have seen EDs who tried to do this, and the result was disastrous for both the Board and the ED. In one situation, the ED's behavior caused a valued Board member to resign as a show of support for the ED. The ED's behavior could have led to a larger schism on the Board if a few other members who had been the ED's supporters hadn't endorsed the decision to terminate.

A variety of signals can indicate that the board has a problem with the ED:

- Consistently rejecting the ED's recommendations.

- Insisting on change just for change's sake.

- Requesting excessive information on a subject before a decision can be made.

- Arguing that things are black when the ED says they're white—particularly when the argument doesn't seem to be on topic. For example, if the Board says the Form 990 wasn't filled out properly when it really was, then the problem likely has to do with something else.

- Becoming more involved in the day-to-day operations.

- Complaining about things that never received the Board's attention before.

- Issuing memorandums of discipline or placing the ED on probation.

The last signal is usually the ultimate message that something is wrong. A memorandum of disciplinary action is usually one of the first tangible signs that the Board is starting to build a case for getting rid of the ED. Being placed on probation is sometimes used as the proverbial two-by-four to get the attention of the ED. At this point the ED needs to decide whether to hold or fold.

The ED should respond to the signals by trying to determine what options are realistic and in the best interest of the organization, as well as what is fair to the ED personally. The ED needs to reflect on issues such as these:

- Are the changes being requested consistent with the organization's mission and values? If not, why not?

- Are the Board's concerns based on facts or perceptions?

- Are the concerns easily fixed?

- Am I capable of changing to the degree being asked of me?

- Is the Board open to discussing the concerns and changing its opinions?

- Are the issues being raised a smoke screen for other problems not mentioned? If so, how can those issues be coaxed into the open?

- Are the concerns expressed held by the full Board or just an influential few?

- Are there ways things can change to the satisfaction of the Board without my leaving?

- What would I have to do to resolve the issues being raised?

The answers to these questions may result in a strong commitment by the ED to respond to the changes being requested and improve the relationship with the Board. The ED's decision to "hold 'em," however, must be accompanied by a strong, realistic perception that if changes occur, the relationship with the Board will greatly improve.

On the other hand, reviewing the situation may prompt the ED to consider "folding 'em" instead. If leaving is in the best interest of the organization, it also must be done on terms that are fair to the ED. The ED should share these reflections with the Board President and seek a fair severance package. Negotiating such a package will depend on the organization's financial status, the presence or lack of a contract, the length of time the ED has been with the organization, and the amount of support for the ED on the Board.

No Surprises, Full Disclosure

Surprises may be fun when you are a child, but they are not the way to enhance a trusting and respectful relationship among grown-ups. No one likes to be surprised when it comes to issues related to their job. When the Board begins to surprise the ED it is usually a clear signal that they have lost their trust, respect, and confidence in the officer's abilities.

We know of one Board President who enjoyed surprising the ED in front of other Board and committee members and staff. The surprises continued for a while and then the ED decided it was time to leave. Whether that was what the Board President wanted or was just her style of leadership, the result ended with the loss of an ED.

Which brings us to another very important point: All relationships should be based on two simple principles:

No Surprises

Full Disclosure

In today's environment, post Enron, WorldCom, United Way of America, and the American Red Cross, the concepts of *no surprises* and *full disclosure* are even more important than ever before.

Knowing when to hold 'em and when to fold 'em is critical, because if the Board or ED make a hasty decision—or if the ED stays on too long—it may not be in the best interest of the organization and may be unfair to the ED. Therefore, it is important for both the Board and the Executive Director to consider each option carefully.

## 2

Preparing for Executive Transition

Boards usually have a plan for their own leadership successions. They have Presidents-elect and Vice Presidents waiting in the wings in the event that the Board President steps down. A well-managed organization has contingency plans for disasters such as fires, floods, and tornadoes, and, since September 11, 2001, even for threats to its very survival. Many organizations have prepared themselves for responding to the media when faced with a public relations crisis.

But when it comes to knowing how to react to the departure of the Executive Director—one of the most significant moments in the organization's life—most nonprofit organizations have no plan at all.

If the departure is announced well in advance—as is sometimes the case with the Gone Fishing Factor—the Board has ample time to draw up a plan, conduct a search, and hire someone new. More often, though, an ED's departure leaves too little time to go through all the steps needed to find the right person and ensure a smooth transition. In those cases, the capacity of an organization to survive and thrive after the loss of the ED depends on its ability to respond quickly and decisively. That is why it is crucial to have a plan already in place.

Transition planning is best done before a crisis—before there's any hint that the ED is leaving—when you have ample time to logically

SOME BOARDS ARE FACED WITH
AN UNEXPECTED EXECUTIVE DEPARTURE

and rationally consider the options available to the organization. Risk management is the name of the game.

When the Board is not prepared for the unexpected exit of the ED, confusion, anxiety, and uncertainty may result. When the Board does have a plan, its members' valuable time will best be spent providing assurance of stability and keeping the organization focused on its mission.

Jan Masaoka, Executive Director of CompassPoint in San Francisco, said this about executive transition: "Why should we think about it? Because we need to be prepared for such crucial moments in our organizations' histories. We prepare (or try to prepare!) for board leadership transition, relocations, changes in funding streams and new accounting guidelines. Executive transition represents a very powerful moment in an organization's life, yet many agencies don't plan or prepare for this pivotal transition" (Bailey, 1997).

Preparing for this "powerful moment" requires that the Board use two approaches, one focused on internal succession planning and the other on external leadership scanning.

Internal Succession Planning

The goal of every ED and Board should be to cultivate the talent of the organization's staff (Carey and Ogden, 2000), and that includes developing a process that enhances the leadership ability of every employee. Leadership enhancement is an investment in the organization's overall success—as well as a prerequisite for succession planning.

To encourage staff members at all levels to assume leadership roles, the leadership needs to delegate decision making and be willing to allocate resources—time and money—to the formal educational process of leadership development.

The use of work teams is one way to provide practical opportunities for problem solving and decision making. The designated team leader is usually referred to as the extrinsic leader. But often other leaders—called intrinsic leaders—will surface within the team.

They are the ones who have significant influence over the other participants. Almost every group has an intrinsic leader, who may or may not be the extrinsic leader. Developing those intrinsic leaders to their greatest potential is the responsibility of every organization and can ultimately lead to cultivation of new, visionary leadership.

As the organization commits to investing in its staff's leadership skills, it must also commit to embracing change and encouraging and supporting risk. And it must accept the idea that failure is an opportunity to learn as part of its commitment to change and leadership enhancement.

Applying these commitments to preparing for the time a successor is needed for the present ED will require a partnership between the Board and the ED. Succession planning requires an open, level playing field with objectivity and fairness throughout the process.

If the organization has the resources, and especially if it has a large staff, it is good practice to have at least two or three top administrators in a position to be considered for the ED's job at any time. Providing these managers opportunities to hone their leadership skills is an essential part of succession planning. The grooming process may include the following opportunities:

- *Attending conferences and seminars that emphasize leadership and management skills.* Professional development goes beyond the skills associated with the services provided by the organization. Too many EDs come out of the rank and file of the program side of operations without having had leadership training. In today's environment of limited resources and increasing demand for accountability and outcomes, the skills of the nonprofit leader need to be based in sound fiscal and management principles and practices. Therefore, many organizations are requiring that their key management team members attend seminars, workshops, and courses that teach them to apply business principles to their positions within the nonprofit organization.

The ever-expanding nonprofit management and leadership programs on major university campuses are a testament to the nonprofit world's recognition that training for EDs is an important market niche. Organizations should be taking advantage of these services.

The ED who does not encourage management team members to expand their skills is not only shortsighted but also sending them the signal that they are not valuable enough to be worth an investment in continued training. The Board in turn must also be committed to the ED's management and leadership development, investing in continuing education and other opportunities for professional growth. Together they need to plan and monitor the organization's leadership development program.

• *Creating occasions for interaction with the Board.* The Board and ED must make a concerted effort to provide opportunities for key leaders of the management staff to interact with various Board members both professionally and socially.

Department heads should be assigned to Board committees that have responsibilities for program or management areas related to their position on the management team. For example, the Chief Financial Officer would meet with the Finance Committee, the Director of Human Resources would provide staff support to the Personnel Committee, and the Director of Development would interact with the Development and Fundraising Committee.

Members of the management team should be invited to attend all Board meetings. A particular area of operations should be highlighted during each Board meeting, thereby creating an opportunity for potential ED candidates to exhibit their reporting and presentation skills, both written and oral.

We have known a number of EDs or Boards with a policy that prohibits members of the management team from attending committee or Board meetings. That only creates or reinforces perceptions of mistrust that either the Board or staff may have of each other. If they cannot attend Board or committee meetings, the management team must rely on the ED for information—and the ED's reports may or may not be accurate.

• *Assigning responsibilities that will demonstrate leadership skills.* Assigning special tasks to various members of the management team challenges them to demonstrate their ability to critically analyze issues of importance. It permits them to expand their usual sphere of influence and show how they can apply, or when necessary change, their style of management. These opportunities should be motivating, designed to stimulate creative problem solving and create opportunities to expand the manager's reputation and influence.

If a manager does not react to an assignment above and beyond the normal workload with enthusiasm and excitement, the individual's status as a potential ED needs to be carefully reevaluated.

• *Mentoring the ED*. The preparation for being an ED does not always come from education, work experiences, or attendance at workshops and conferences. Some of the best learning comes from the guidance and mentoring of skilled and nurturing Board members.

One ED we know was having problems at home with a difficult marriage and a chronically ill child. She was feeling totally inadequate. This feeling of being overwhelmed was spilling over into her work. She was seriously considering preparing her three envelopes. When she was invited out for lunch by the Board's top three officers, all highly successful business leaders in the community, our ED friend was prepared for the news that her tenure was being terminated.

Instead, the three Board members informed her that they were convinced she was still the best person for the ED's job and that they were pledging their willingness to invest their time to help her develop the necessary skills. Her success depended on her willingness to commit to the hard work they were going to design for her. She agreed enthusiastically.

Over the next few years she attended numerous business seminars on topics such as strategic thinking and planning, analytical assessment and evaluation, personnel motivation, outcome management, and product quality enhancement. She read books on leadership and management that were on a long list provided by the three mentors. She met with each of the three individually and together at least once a month for a debriefing and feedback.

Overall the work was hard but exciting, and as she applied her new skills, the organization grew and became more stable. The three mentors had accomplished their goal, an ED who was both a leader and a manager. Meanwhile, as the ED's feelings of self-worth and accomplishment increased, her ability to cope with her child's illness greatly improved, and the child is now thriving with a more confident mother. The marriage did not survive, however. Even the most rewarding work can't solve every problem!

External Leadership

When considering succession planning, most organizations think only in terms of their internal preparation, as just described. Organizations also need to think outside their own box.

Many potential leaders in other organizations should be kept on the Board's radar screen: Executive Directors, Board members, or middle managers of competing or complementing organizations. When Board members keep track of people outside their own organization who have demonstrated their readiness to assume a greater role and responsibility in leadership, the pool of candidates is much larger than when they keep their eyes on their own staff. And the pool of candidates grows exponentially when the Board and ED work together to identify leaders in other organizations. The more potential leaders the Board can identify—both internally and externally—the better prepared the organization will be for the inevitable change.

Understanding and Managing the Phenomenon of Change

A wonderful Gary Larson "Far Side" cartoon depicts a significant moment for mankind. Picture this: Three cavemen huddle around a fire holding their food over the flames in their hands. In the background a fourth caveman is holding his food over his fire at the end of a stick. One of the three cavemen exclaims in excitement, "Hey! Look what Zog do!" *A paradigm shift has occurred.*

Sage and Burrello (1994), writing about managing change in the field of special education, advised, "For a change process to begin, there must be creative tension between the current reality and future alternatives." This observation can be easily applied to the challenges of preparing for and managing the changes that occur during executive transition.

Everyone reacts to change differently. Because no one is sure of the future during executive transition, the changes may make Board, staff, consumers, funders, and other stakeholders uncomfortable. Fear of the unknown can make anyone anxious. On the other hand, some may react with optimism, viewing a change in leadership as an opportunity.

Ways of Dealing with Change

Because the Board must guide the organization through the transition, it should step back and try to understand how its own

WHEN AN EXECUTIVE DIRECTOR LEAVES
UNEXPECTANTLY, EXPECT THE ENTIRE
STAFF TO FEEL DISPLACED

members—as well as staff, funders, and other stakeholders—respond to change. We have identified four general approaches to change:

- The Ostrich Approach

- The "I Won't Move" Approach

- The Scarlet O'Hara Approach

- The Star Ship *Enterprise* Approach

The Ostrich Approach

Ostriches have a reputation for hiding their heads in the sand when threatened, hoping the cause of the danger will pass and leave them unharmed. As erroneous as the description is, it illustrates the way many organizations and individuals respond to the idea of change. Change may be inevitable, but most people are unprepared for it. Not accepting the inevitability of change may result in being left behind.

The Ostrich Approach in executive transition is visible when the majority of Board members deny that the ED is underperforming (the Cutting the Mustard Factor), or when they fail to recognize or respond when the ED is starting to react to the stress of the job (the Burnout Factor). Even if Board members do recognize the issue, they often hope the problem will go away with little or no intervention.

We know of one organization that had to be awakened by their primary funding source to the fact that their ED was not providing appropriate leadership. The funder had expressed its concerns to the ED numerous times. Program outcomes were not clearly defined or measured. Program and financial reports were always late and inaccurate. After almost eighteen months of tolerating the problem, the funder met with the Board and announced that the ED had to go or it would withdraw its funding. Some members of the Board claimed they were taken by surprise. Others acknowledged that they were aware of the inadequacies but did not raise the issue because they did not want to "rock the boat." By hiding its head in the sand, the organization almost lost its primary funding source. The wake-up call resulted in a change of leadership, just in time.

The "I Won't Move" Approach

Resistance to change is as inevitable as change itself. Resistance may come in many forms, from blatant and up front to insidious and hidden. Dealing with resistance to executive change takes different forms depending on the factor that caused the change, but no matter which of the seven factors caused the departure of the ED, the organization may experience resistance from staff, stakeholders, and Board members. As the old saying goes, "No matter how messed up we are, there are always those who don't want to see any changes."

An example of the "I Won't Move" Approach is the ED who had been with the organization over ten years (Ten Year Factor). She had been receiving performance evaluations from the Board's Executive Committee over the past three years that were less than satisfactory. The new Executive Committee restated the same concerns expressed before and set goals that they wanted the organization to accomplish under the ED's leadership. The ED did not take these expectations seriously, rationalizing that the Board members involved in setting the goals were unrealistic in their vision for the organization.

The Board offered the ED all types of resources and support to assist her in making the changes. But she had weathered similar efforts of other executive committees and felt she would outlast this group also. The situation came to a head and the Board decided to let her go and find a new ED whose vision for the organization was similar to theirs.

The Scarlet O'Hara Approach

Remember Scarlet flittering around, waving her hands and exclaiming, "Oh fiddle-dee-dee, I'll worry about *that* tomorrow"? Putting off responding to the need to change is just as bad as ignoring it or digging in your heels—it will only compound the problem.

As the tension increases, solutions to the "future alternatives" usually only get more complex and harder to implement. Putting off the need to change is like removing a bandage slowly—it's harder and more painful.

Once the decision is made to start the executive transition process, it is best to begin the course of action quickly so the organization can accept the change, make the adjustment, and get on with its mission.

The Star Ship *Enterprise* Approach

The best approach to reacting to change is to boldly go forward where no organization has gone before. The crew of the *Enterprise* encountered many challenges and experienced numerous adventures. Change provides the excitement of new opportunities.

Price Pritchett, author of *Culture Shift: The Employee Handbook for Changing Corporate Culture* (1993), says we should respond to change like children:

- Be flexible.

- Seek variety.

- Be inquisitive.

- Be willing to take risks.

- Ask questions.

- Have no inhibitions.

- Accept new challenges.

You may have heard the story of the twins confronted with a pile of manure. One twin sat down in the corner and began to cry in disappointment; the other grabbed a shovel and began digging. When asked what he was doing, he replied, "With all this manure there has to be a pony in here somewhere."

We need to be like the optimistic twin. When faced with the inevitability of change, organizations and EDs should look for those future alternatives through traditional and nontraditional methods. Change should motivate the search for new visions.

The Rules of Change

In addition to understanding how people respond to change, it is important to recognize certain truths about change. As discussed earlier, executive transition is one of the most significant changes an organization will ever experience. It is therefore important to understand the phenomenon of change in general—its effect on individuals and organizations and how it can be managed in the context of executive transition.

Change Is Uncomfortable

Change makes us uneasy. We prefer the familiar. To demonstrate, fold your hands, interlinking your fingers and determine which thumb is on top. Unfold your hands and refold them consciously putting the opposite thumb on top. Don't be surprised if you feel uncomfortable. You have changed something that is familiar and comfortable and that change has caused you to feel awkward.

We have already discussed the concept of knowing when to hang on and knowing when to make a change. Hesitating to make the tough decision of either leaving a bad situation or terminating an ineffective ED is an example of not wanting to change because it is unpleasant and challenging. People sometimes would prefer to put up with problems rather than make a change. But as Karl Albrecht, author of *The Only Thing That Matters* (1992), reminds us:

> If you always do
> what you always did,
> you'll always get
> what you always got.

Change Can Be Costly

No matter what creates change, it can be costly. It can require financial resources to restructure operations, retool for new opportunities, or increase the commitment to the vision and mission by starting new services. The organization may go over budget to cover transition services such as interim management or an executive search firm.

Financial resources may be required to support management's effort to maintain the morale and performance level of staff. The organization may establish a system of recognizing outstanding performances through rewards and bonuses. Some organizations have an annual picnic for staff and volunteers. We have worked with organizations that give staff tickets to the movies or coupons for dinner for two at a nice restaurant. Something as simple as sandwiches at staff meetings can make a big difference in staff morale. We are not talking about first-class tickets to Europe, but small perks need to be in the budget. If staff morale suffers, productivity may decline, affecting the organization's ability to produce its services cost-effectively. The services provided may also be affected qualitatively, since staff may become careless, increasing incidents at the operational and program level.

To respond to these issues, the administration will need to increase its oversight of finances and programs. Supervisors need to be more specific in their directions. Staff members need to stay focused on what they are doing. Priorities need to be redefined with an emphasis on short-term objectives. Deadlines and time lines help keep the work on track, and setting performance targets with defined milestones for achievement can be helpful.

Just when the organization is spending more money because of the transition, fundraising may be adversely affected. Investors may be hesitant to make commitments until the organization has demonstrated it can successfully manage the challenges of having lost its leader. This is the time when Board leadership needs to assure investors that the transition is providing an opportunity for renewed energy and a renewed focus on the organization's mission. Investors have to be encouraged not only to maintain their level of support but also to consider increasing it to offset costs associated with the transition.

Change Requires Communication

Throughout the transition process, communication is key, and we will continue to emphasize that point throughout this book. If the response to change is driven by anxiety about the unknown, then knowledge is an important weapon against resistance to change. Information comes from communication.

How the organization shares information with stakeholders is important. A factual memorandum to staff from the Board President may not be the best option. If everyone is grieving over the sudden death of a respected leader, it may be better to invite staff to a prayer meeting to support one another. Other forms of gathering may be the best response to other crises of leadership, including acrimonious departures or legal difficulties. This provides an opportunity for the Board to demonstrate their feelings of loss and concern. The Board President can offer a few words of assurance that the Board is mobilized to respond to the leadership void and more details will be forthcoming. A follow-up letter or memorandum can be sent in a few days with more specific information on how the Board is proceeding to assure the staff and other stakeholders that the organization will get through the challenge. The staff and stakeholders should get periodic updates about the progress of the transition.

The Board should pay special attention to key investors during this time, using individual meetings, telephone calls, e-mail messages, and personal letters. This will be helpful during the transition, but it will be especially helpful in the future, since it will demonstrate how well the organization dealt with a difficult situation and that the investor was recognized as an important stakeholder.

Communication comes in different forms. How the organization behaves during a leadership crisis is another very important way to communicate how the executive transition is affecting the organization. Emphasizing program successes is an excellent way to demonstrate that the organization's services are continuing as usual. Marketing and public relations efforts need to be focused and increased. Maintaining traditional activities during this period—such as adhering to the calendar of events—demonstrates that although the ED may be changing, other activities will continue as usual.

Change Offers the Opportunity to Create Something Better

It may seem obvious but change should be used to take what is and turn it into what should be. Executive transition offers a wonderful opportunity to review the organization at all levels and develop a plan for making improvements. The result of the evaluation will help the Board clarify the direction of the organization, which in turn simplifies the process of identifying the expertise and skill sets needed by the next ED.

Most Boards will understand that a change in ED provides the opportunity to move the organization to a higher and better level of performance financially and programmatically. What Board members should also recognize is that with a new ED their roles and responsibilities may be challenged and require change. As a new staff leader is about to arrive on the scene, the Board should take this time to go through a self-evaluation of its roles and responsibilities and how it shares organizational leadership with the ED.

In conclusion, we suggest that the word *change* itself provides the guidelines we have been discussing in this chapter.

Change Is Inevitable

This may sound trite, but it is very important. If the concept of inevitable change is not at the heart of the organization's culture, the

Board and staff will have to deal with internal resistance when any change is attempted. Encouraging change creates an atmosphere in which everyone in the organization will be a change leader.

One organization we know brings the possibility of change into every Board and staff meeting. The possibility of a different or a better way is part of every discussion. Questions such as "If we could change one thing about how we are approaching this problem, what would we do differently?" are frequently asked. Also asked are questions about the possibility of unwelcome changes, such as "Is there anything that could come along and really sideswipe this program?" As a result, the staff and Board feel comfortable with looking at all sides of an issue and are more fully engaged than their counterparts in most organizations.

Have a Plan—Be Proactive

Don't wait for changes in the environment to dictate your destiny. Create the vision of how the organization should look ten years from now. Identify the inhibitors and facilitators to fulfilling the vision. Develop strategies to address factors that will enhance the chances of success.

Board retreats are an excellent way to explore the vision of the future. Some organizations choose to look twenty years out, others choose five or ten years. It is amazing how different the visions of different stakeholders can be. When we did a visioning session for a performing arts group, we found that some Board members envisioned a school attached to the organization, others wanted a touring company, and still others wanted a larger performance space. Discussing the vision of the future clarifies the organization's direction and influences decisions related to recruiting and hiring a new ED.

Anticipate Changes in the Industry

Stay informed. Read the literature of the field and of related fields. Keep on top of changes in public policy and evaluate their potential impact on the organization. Seek information from the organization's stakeholders and how they perceive its services and future needs. Do not attempt to predict the future without looking at the present.

Network with Key Stakeholders

Change cannot be implemented successfully in a vacuum. It must involve everyone connected with the organization, including staff, funders, investors, public policymakers, and other complementing and competing organizations. Seeking support and assistance is not a sign of weakness but an indication of reality in today's environment. Strategic alliances are usually formed in order to benefit all their members. Don't be afraid to ask for help from your friends.

Give Change a Chance

Don't give up too soon on the innovation. When planning a new program or approach, include a shakedown period in the time line. Allow for trial and error and accept slow progress and setbacks as part of the learning curve. Remember: Being innovative means taking risks—and learning from mistakes.

Evaluate the Impact of the Changes

Organizations need to build into their change plan a way to track how the changes are measuring up against projected outcomes. Change for change's sake should never be implemented. Changes should enhance a service, improve the efficiency of the organization, or increase the capacity or quality of the programs. Knowing if the change has met expectations will encourage future change projects. Success in one area encourages innovation and risk taking in other areas.

In short, no one can stop the winds of change, but you can be prepared to adjust your sails to maximize its power.

4

Responding to Executive Transition

The second component of the executive transition process is responding to the knowledge that the organization has lost its Executive Director. The void in staff leadership can be both frightening and exhilarating, and the Board needs to consider not only its own response but also the response of the staff, funders, consumers, and other stakeholders.

A sound response system includes four important steps:

1. Initial reaction: *Don't panic—but do something!*
2. Reassure staff, funders, and other stakeholders.
3. Appoint an ad hoc committee.
4. Review the organization's strengths and challenges.

Step #1: Initial Reaction

Don't panic—but do something! Most Boards have a sense of urgency when they learn the ED is leaving or has left. They should not panic and—most important—not make hasty decisions. We have seen too many Boards move too quickly by appointing interim management without considering all options and start looking for a new ED without laying a sound foundation for the search. Thomas Gilmore, in *Making a Leadership Change* (1988), described many

Boards' reactions as "sleep walking" through the transition process. This is not the time to move blindly. It is the time to move forward deliberately and strategically.

We have also worked with others who are frozen in time and unable to budge. Inaction can be just as harmful as hasty decisions. Indecision creates uncertainty, which spurs rumors and speculation among key stakeholders. Speculation and rumors only add to confusion and a feeling of being out of control, and that is the last thing the organization needs.

Inaction also creates a leadership void, so anyone can grab power. The power needs to rest with the Board, until it decides how best to assign it.

The Board's reaction is determined, to some degree, by the circumstances prompting the ED to leave. For example, if the ED is leaving because of the Gone Fishing Factor or the Godfather Factor, the departure probably involves relatively little disruption to the organization and anxiety among stakeholders. Thus the transition process should be fairly simple and easy.

If the ED is leaving under circumstances that are less than amicable or caused by some tragic occurrence (say, the Sudden Loss Factor or the Cutting the Mustard Factor), the situation is much more complex and has the potential to significantly disrupt the organization. The Board's first concern must be the security of the agency's assets. It should initiate the following activities within the first few days after the ED's departure.

- Change signatures, passwords, and PINs (personal identification numbers) on all bank accounts, safe-deposit boxes, money accounts, credit cards, and the like.

- Change locks on internal and external office doors and vehicles if deemed appropriate.

- Change passwords for access to computer software.

- Change e-mail address.

- Change the ED's voice-mail message.

Step #2: Reassure Staff, Funders, and Other Stakeholders

Regardless of the reason for the executive transition, another primary responsibility of the Board is to assure staff and other stakeholders that the organization is under control and someone is in charge. This will require a public relations strategy for responding to questions regarding the departure of the ED and announcing the ED transition. The Board must keep all stakeholders informed of what has happened and what is being planned so the organization will be perceived as well managed and governed by a strong and involved Board of Directors. The key here is *communicate, communicate, communicate*.

Staff

The Board should periodically meet with the agency's management team members. Good communication will help keep your best swimmers from jumping ship. Most important, it will assure that services are not interrupted.

The Board should try to anticipate the staff's response to the transition in leadership and take steps to keep employee morale high throughout the process. Staff may exhibit sadness or gladness, depending on their perception of the departing ED and the factors precipitating the transition. The transition may increase or decrease employee trust or mistrust in the Board. To neglect staff's feelings during this time will create numerous problems for the interim ED and the incoming ED.

Funders

Funders don't like to be surprised or to find out from others that an organization is having a problem or in the midst of change. Transparency needs to be the guiding philosophy. If possible, key investors should be alerted to any change before it occurs, but if that is not possible, they should be told immediately afterward.

They need to be assured that the organization is stable and that the services they fund will continue to be provided. They may also get involved in funding the search process—and the interim ED, if one is necessary—to ensure their investment is protected.

Funders may make inquiries as to the status of the projects in which they have invested. They may make demands that signal their uneasiness, such as wanting to see a rehearsal if they're funding an arts organization, reviewing raw data if the work involves a research component, and generally requesting to be more in the loop than with previously funded projects. The Board needs to be responsive to these requests.

Other Stakeholders

Others in the community may perceive the organization as being vulnerable during a transition. Competition for good employees, funds, consumers, and volunteers is always a reality of life for any nonprofit organization. Competitors may attempt to divert manpower and financial resources from the organization in transition to themselves. Therefore it is important to portray the image of confidence and stability throughout the process. Being decisive, organized, and open throughout the period of change conveys an image of strength.

Throughout the process, it is essential for the Board to speak with one voice through a designated spokesperson. This may include who addresses the press, the public, and the funders or clients. Sometimes the spokesperson might be a staffer, a Board member, or even a celebrity invited to speak for the organization. What's important is that everyone understands their roles and responsibilities. No rumors, no innuendoes, and *no surprises*.

Step #3: Appoint an Ad Hoc Committee

One of the best ways to assure a well-coordinated transition is for the Board to appoint an ad hoc Executive Transition Committee. Committee members may include members and nonmembers of the

Board. Individuals such as Human Resource Directors from local businesses make excellent committee members.

The committee should develop the strategies for appointing interim management, if needed, and implementing an executive search process. The committee is the workhorse of the Board. It brings recommendations to the Board for final ratification.

Step #4: Review the Organization's Strengths and Challenges

Organizations are sometimes in great disarray at the time of transition. It is important that the organization use this time of change to assess its strengths and problems, looking for opportunities and threats.

Assessing the organization's vision, mission, core values, policies, and operating procedures will help the Board when it needs to identify the characteristics, expertise, and skill sets of the new ED, and it will also help the new ED take the reins.

For example, the Board should consider the following questions:

- Are the fiscal matters of the organization in compliance with generally accepted accounting practices, and have recent auditors' recommendations been implemented?

- What is the corporate culture of the organization, including personnel policies and procedures?

- What is the staff's prevailing perception of the organization and its operations?

- Are the organization's services compatible with its mission and is it still meeting a community need? Are its programs producing the anticipated outcomes?

- How do the funders (private and public) perceive the value of their investment in the organization?

- Does the Board function in the most efficient and effective manner possible?

- What governance and Board policies and procedures need to be reviewed and possibly improved?

- What was the Board's relationship with the outgoing ED? Is there a need to redefine how the Board relates to the next ED?

Executive transition may provide an opportune time to conduct an independent, objective institutional audit. The Board may come to the conclusion that internal changes need to be made at various levels. Identifying where changes need to be made and how to implement them will require a timetable and specific task assignments.

It is usually not good practice to make substantial changes to the organization's operations during times of leadership change. Conducting a full strategic planning process, for example, is rarely appropriate at this time but should be on the radar screen for when the new ED has been hired and on the job for three to six months. However, if the organization is faced with a potential financial or programmatic crisis, structural changes to operations may be required immediately. Implementing those changes may be the responsibility of the Board or the appointed interim ED. Remember the story of the three envelopes in the Preface and the advice of the second envelope? The organization does not have to wait for the next ED to consider reorganizing, relocating, or merging.

How the Board responds to the fears of staff and stakeholders and approaches the initial challenges to executive transition will have an impact on determining the opportunities that become available.

Whatever the challenge, always remember that there is lemonade hidden in those lemons—all you need to do is squeeze it out of them.

5

Appointing an Interim Executive Director

Unless the current ED announces an impending departure well in advance—or unless the Board has a successor waiting in the wings—an organization may need an interim Executive Director for some period of time. Appointing an interim ED is as critical a decision as selecting a permanent ED and may have consequences that will affect the organization both immediately and in the future.

The interim ED is a caretaker, holding things together until the permanent ED arrives on the scene, but can also be much more. An interim ED can provide a bridge between the previous executive and the next, helping the Board, staff, and other stakeholders adjust to the fact that the previous ED is no longer there. The interim leader can prepare the organization for changes that will occur with the new leadership and play an important role in demonstrating that change can provide new opportunities for the organization.

If the organization finds itself facing significant administrative and management issues that need to be addressed right away, the interim ED can also be like a Sheriff's deputy—the one responsible for law and order in the town while the Sheriff is away. The deputy sees that the saloon has been taking advantage of the cowboys with watered-down whiskey and crooked gambling tables. If something isn't done soon, the cowboys are threatening to shoot up the town. So the deputy has a heart-to-heart with the barkeep.

SOMETIMES AN INTERIM IS YOUR BEST
CHOICE TO RESTORE LAW AND ORDER

The interim ED needs to have the freedom to initiate change and resolve issues that threaten the efficient operation of the organization. At the same time, the interim ED has the obligation to keep the Board leadership informed of the problems discovered and the corrections planned.

The use of an interim ED is not a new concept. Various religious organizations routinely assign interim ministers when a minister leaves a pulpit. The congregation may go through a grieving process and the interim minister can help church members work through their anger, fear, and sorrow, eventually reaching acceptance. The interim minister is also there to help the congregation get ready to adjust to a new minister's style. These two roles provide the important foundation for the next permanent minister to come in and succeed.

These are the general roles and responsibilities of the interim ED:

- Provide oversight and management of the organization's operations, including protection of the organization's capital assets.

    Provide oversight of the organization's fiscal affairs, ensuring tight budget controls.

    Ensure that the organization's services and programs continue as scheduled and maintain their efficiency and quality.

    Provide technical and professional support to the organization's Board and its committees.

- Ensure the stability and morale of the staff.

- Maintain lines of communication with key stakeholders, assuring funders, consumers, and others that the agency is in experienced hands.

    Represent the organization in the community.

- Prepare the organization for the next ED.

- Assume other duties as dictated by the organization's needs.

  Submit weekly activity and status reports to the Board President.

  Remain accessible to the Board President and staff.

Appointing Interim Transition Management

The Transition Committee should assume responsibility to consider its options regarding the appointment of an interim ED, but it is the Board's responsibility to make the final decision regarding appointing interim transition management.

One of the first things the Board should develop, in conjunction with the Transition and Finance Committees, is an executive transition budget. This should take into account how much the organization can spend for the appointment of an interim ED and how much can it spend on the executive search.

The Transition Committee should construct a list of the interim's responsibilities and identify the lines of supervision. (Who does the interim report to and who reports to the interim?) It will also need to determine how long the interim is likely to be needed (probably four to six months or perhaps longer). In addition, the committee needs to determine if the organization needs a full-time or part-time interim ED. This determination will depend on whether the interim is to be a caretaker, an evaluator, or an evaluator and change agent.

The Transition Committee should create questions for use when interviewing the candidates. Some general questions may include

- How would you describe your management style?

- How would people you've supervised describe your management style?

- What do you believe is the difference between an ED and an interim ED?

- If you were a member of the Board of Directors, what would you expect of the interim ED?

- What are the first five things you would do as interim ED?

Fairly early in the process, the committee should also decide what role, if any, the interim should have in the executive search.

When choosing an interim Executive Director, the Board has three options:

- Appoint a member of the existing management team.

- Appoint a current member or past member of the Board.

- Retain the services of an independent professional interim ED.

It is important for the committee to carefully consider the advantages, disadvantages, and consequences associated with each option. The following sections describe these points, and also list more specific questions to ask when interviewing staff, Board members, or outside candidates for the position.

A Member of the Management Staff

Selecting a current staff member as an interim offers a number of advantages. It will provide continuity, as the staff member will be familiar with the agency's clients, services, procedures, and policies, and with its culture—and is already known to the Board. Depending on the role of the staff person, the candidate may be familiar with the funding sources supporting the agency. Having someone acquainted with the organization's operations may make it more likely that the organization will meet established deadlines and that events already planned will continue as scheduled.

Appointing a member of the staff usually means choosing someone who can assume the duties of the ED immediately. If the departure is abrupt or chaotic, an existing staffer can make the transition a little less bumpy.

Another advantage of hiring a member of the staff is that that person's salary is already in the budget, though the Board will need to consider additional compensation such as a bonus for the interim as well as funds to cover services for the appointee's added responsibilities. The economies associated with appointing an interim from within are particularly important if the reason for departure of the previous ED involves fiscal mismanagement or crisis, in which case available funds might be insufficient for hiring someone from outside.

Selecting a current staff member as an interim also has some disadvantages. The organization might not have anyone on its management team ready to assume the ED's responsibilities. Beware of the "Peter Principle," which states that people rise to their level of incompetence—the obvious candidate for promotion might be taking that last fatal step beyond the top.

Appointing a member of the existing staff makes it necessary to find someone to fill that individual's regular responsibilities. In addition, other staff members may be jealous, angry, fearful, or disappointed at the elevation of a peer to the interim job, and they may resist this person's authority or try to take advantage of previous relationships.

Having a member of the staff lead an organizational system or structural change process would not be appropriate. In most cases an individual selected from the staff may have been involved in developing the system, and therefore may not be able to objectively evaluate its functionality.

And appointing a staff member may pose a dilemma if someone else is chosen for the permanent job: Consider the consequences if the appointed interim ED submits a résumé for the permanent position and does not get it. What will happen next? Will the interim go back to the previous staff position and still feel good about the job and organization? Experience shows that it is difficult for anyone to retreat to a former position. Relationships with peers and the Board may have changed, creating potential conflicts and ill feelings.

Another consequence may be that the rejected individual may develop a perception of having no future with the organization and therefore conclude that it is time to leave the agency.

The result may be the loss of a good staff person. And if the former interim does decide to stay, how will that individual respond to the new ED? Is it realistic to expect someone in that position to welcome the new ED? There is a good probability the staff person may be uncooperative.

How will the new ED feel about having the former interim ED on staff? The new ED may feel that the staff person is second-guessing decisions and undermining the center of authority. The process of acclimating oneself to a new job—and in some instances a new community—is challenging enough without a potential Brutus within the organization.

Additional Issues to Consider

Appointing a staff member as interim ED raises a number of questions that need to be considered to capitalize on the potential advantages and reduce the impact of the disadvantages.

Compensation. The Transition Committee needs to consider fair compensation for the employee who will be the interim ED. The committee may want to establish a formula that will provide guidance on how to recognize the employee's increase in responsibilities. It may be the difference between the employee's present salary and the base salary of the departing ED. The employee may be given 25 percent, 50 percent, 75 percent, or 100 percent of the difference. (The committee may want to consider using the salary range being considered for the new ED in this formula, rather than the salary of the previous ED.)

The committee may want to designate the salary differential as a bonus or may want to add it to base salary while someone is serving as interim ED. A bonus may be given on a monthly basis or at the end of the interim's tenure. A bonus would not affect the organization's contribution to the employee's 401(K) or 403(b) retirement plan, nor would it affect disability insurance or other similar benefits.

Covering Current Responsibilities. The committee should work with the employee on a strategy to ensure that the responsibilities of the interim's permanent position are being met. This may require assigning responsibilities to other management team members. Another alternative may be to spread the workload among other staff members or to bring in an outside temporary staffer (such as a grant writer, special events professional, or administrative assistant) to fill the gap.

Involvement with ED Search. It would not be appropriate for the interim ED to participate in the search process if that individual is an announced candidate for the position. An appointed interim ED who has indicated unwillingness to be considered for the permanent position could appropriately participate in the search process, as discussed in Chapter Six. The interim ED will bring a unique perspective that may be helpful for both the Search Committee and the candidates.

Responsibilities and Expectations. The roles and responsibilities for an interim ED selected from the organization's staff should be limited to being a caretaker, maintaining the organization's day-to-day operations. It is not appropriate for a staff-member interim ED to be a change agent.

Reporting Relationships. The interim ED will interact with all members of the Board and its committee chairs. The overall supervisory line of communication should be with one member of the Board, who is customarily the President. The Board President and interim ED should maintain a close working relationship, which may require daily or at least weekly communication.

The interim should provide the Board President with a detailed written report on all activities during the previous week. The report could also include a list of activities planned for the following week.

Supervisory Relationships. The interim ED usually supervises those employees who reported to the previous ED. This requires the appointed employee to supervise peers and colleagues. This, as discussed earlier, may be a problem for the interim or the other staff members, or both. Therefore, the interim's role as supervisor may be more as a coach or mentor, rather than a boss. The interim should not have the authority to hire or fire management team members without approval from the Board's Executive Committee or the full Board.

Term of Appointment. The interim ED should be appointed with the intent of holding that position for as long as it takes to find a new ED. But the appointment is at the discretion of the Board, so the interim may be removed from the position at any time. The individual's return to the former job will depend on the reasons for being removed from the interim position.

If the interim has violated the organization's policies and is removed for cause, as defined in the organization's personnel policies, then termination from employment with the organization is appropriate. If the Board or Transition Committee determines that the interim ED's position is not within someone's capabilities, then it is appropriate to restore the previous position without prejudice.

Specific Questions. In addition to the general questions recommended earlier in this chapter, the Transition Committee should consider asking a candidate who is a member of the staff these questions:

- How would you would relate to the other members
  of the management team once you were appointed
  as interim ED?

- What do you think your relationship will be with your
  peers and colleagues when you return to your present
  position?

- How would you propose to ensure that your present
  responsibilities be fulfilled if you are appointed
  interim ED?

- Are you interested in being considered for the permanent ED position?

  > If yes: Have you given any thought to how you will
  > respond if the position is given to someone else?
  > If no: Why not?

Letter of Appointment

The committee should confirm the appointment through a written
memorandum or letter that specifies those areas and issues that both
parties have agreed to. The confirmation communiqué should define
the amount of compensation adjustment agreed upon with the staff
member and the scope of work to be accomplished for that compensation. The letter should also specify the projected time line and
time commitments for the interim assignment. The letter of appointment needs to clarify who reports to the interim and to whom
the interim should report. There may need to be some reference to
how the individual's regular work responsibilities will be distributed
among the remaining management team.

A Present or Past Member of the Board

A member of the Board may be available for a short time, thereby
allowing the Board the opportunity to organize itself and consider
all other options for interim management and ultimately who is
hired. The present or past Board member knows the agency and has

a working relationship with the members of the Board and staff. The organization may be fortunate enough to find a Board member who will provide these services pro bono. In addition staff, funders, and clients may know this person and may have a higher comfort level than with an interim from outside the organization.

With a member of the Board in the role of the interim, the Board may obtain a better insight to the scope of the ED's job and the talents and skills necessary. It will also get a more objective review of existing staff's strengths and weaknesses. Appointing a Board member as interim leaves less chance that that person will apply for the vacancy, eliminating conflicts of interest or problems with staff relations.

Appointing someone with Board experience is not without its disadvantages, however. As a general rule, Board members, as policymakers, should not involve themselves in day-to-day operations. A Board member who becomes involved in management may find it difficult to return to a governance role. Moving back from how things are done to what should be done may present challenges for the Board member and the rest of the Board.

As the interim ED, the Board member is the boss, responsible for making operational changes that are perceived as essential to the organization's efficiency and effectiveness. But when the individual returns to the Board and the new ED takes over, the former interim may have difficulty accepting further changes made by the new Executive Director, which could result in tension between the Board member and ED. That tension may even transfer to other Board members, potentially eroding the ED's standing with the Board.

There are times when Boards have appointed a present or past member as interim ED and then decided to make the job permanent. Such appointments have about the same chance of success as any other appointment. There are, however, potential minefields associated with such a decision.

If the Board member who was appointed interim ED offers to take the full-time position, some of the other Board members may think such an offer is not in the best interest of the organization, but may find it difficult to decline their colleague's offer. Differing opinions among Board members on how to respond may create a schism within the Board that may have long-term ramifications. The rejected individual may resign, causing the organization to lose a good Board member, or may stay on but become a major antagonist for the new ED.

If the Board member does take the ED position, it could blur the demarcation of roles and responsibilities between staff leadership and the Board, since Board members are accustomed to interacting with one another as peers. Both the Board and the new ED may have difficulty maintaining the friendly yet professional distance essential to a healthy working relationship.

The Board may have a tendency to abdicate its responsibilities as the governance arm and as policymakers, and to rubber-stamp the ED's recommendations and actions. This may happen because Board members perceive the ED as "one of their own" and are reluctant to question or challenge any proposals the ED may make.

Additional Issues to Consider

Appointing a Board member as interim ED also raises a number of questions that need to be considered.

Compensation. The Board member may be in a financial position to assume the role of interim ED for no compensation. In that case, the Board may want to establish a policy on the personal out-of-pocket expenses for which it will reimburse the interim ED. We are familiar with a national organization in which a member of the Board volunteered to be interim ED for no salary or benefits. However, he lived out of town, so he needed a temporary place to live and felt it was excessive to have to rent a place so he could serve the organization pro bono. The organization paid for those expenses. It was an extremely successful solution.

The Transition Committee may not be able to find a Board member (present or past) in a position to be interim ED without compensation. If that is the case, the committee must negotiate a compensation package that meets the needs of the individual and the organization's budget. For example, if the individual wants to limit income for tax or Social Security reasons, the committee could provide health and dental insurance, or a leased vehicle or car allowance. The Board candidate may identify other nonsalary compensation options.

If the Board member requests compensation for being interim ED the question of continuing service on the Board may need to be considered.

Continuing or Terminating Position on the Board. When a Board member is going to be compensated as interim ED, it may violate the organization's bylaws or a state law about Board member compensation. The Transition Committee should seek legal advice before finalizing any arrangement.

It may be necessary for the Board member to take a leave of absence or resign from the Board. If the need for an interim ED is projected to be three months or less, the Board member may want to ask permission to take leave of absence from the Board. If an interim ED is needed for more than three to six months, the Board member should resign from the Board. At the end of the term as interim ED, the Board member should be eligible to return to the Board at the next scheduled election.

Involvement with ED Search. Any interim ED who is interested in the permanent ED's position should not be actively involved in the ED search process. The person may be asked to assist by developing information on the position's responsibilities and challenges that might be encountered.

However, as with a staff member, a Board interim who is not interested in being a candidate for the permanent position may be included in the executive search. The interim will bring a unique perspective that may be helpful for both the Search Committee and candidates.

Responsibilities and Expectations. In addition to the list of roles and responsibilities already noted, the Transition Committee may want to discuss the possibility of having the Board member who is appointed interim ED observe, analyze, and recommend changes to the organization's operations, policies, and procedures. The extent the Board member interim ED may be used to perform these responsibilities depends upon the individual's skills, experience, and ability to be objective.

The Board may give the interim ED the authority to implement all or some of the changes before the new ED is on the job. Alternatively, the Board may prefer to wait for the new ED to be hired before any substantial changes are implemented. The ED's report could be an important guide for the new ED.

Reporting Relationships. How the interim ED appointed from the ranks of the Board or past Board is supervised presents a challenge to the current Board President. Supervision, in the traditional sense, is not appropriate, but the appointed interim ED should be required to maintain a line of communication with the Board President and the rest of the Board. Weekly reports similar to the ones described for the staff member appointed to the interim job would be appropriate.

Supervisory Relationships. The interim ED usually supervises those employees who reported to the previous ED. The interim should not have the authority to hire or fire management team members without approval from the Board's Executive Committee or the full Board.

Term of Appointment. The interim ED needs to commit to the time necessary to complete the transition process. The commitment required would depend on whether day-to-day operations are functioning well or beset by systemic problems that need correcting.

Whatever this commitment, the interim ED must be in the office and be visible at the organization's programs. An absentee interim ED is not acceptable. On-site leadership and management is essential during the critical phases of the transition from one ED to another.

Interviews. Interviewing possible Board members for the interim ED position should be left to the Transition Committee. How the interview process is conducted will be determined by who is approaching whom. If the committee is approaching the Board member, the process is informal and the conversation is a discussion of issues rather than a set of questions and answers. If the Board member is applying for the position, then the process may take on the format of a more formal interview process.

Regardless of the circumstances, the committee should be sensitive to the unique situation and conduct the process more as a discussion than an interview. The Transition Committee needs to be sensitive to the possibility that it may decide not to appoint the Board member. Rejecting a Board member needs to be done with great sensitivity and finesse to preserve ongoing working relationships.

Specific Questions. In addition to the general questions recommended earlier in this chapter, the Transition Committee should consider asking a candidate who is a present or past member of the Board these questions:

- How much time can you devote to being the interim ED?

- How long can you serve as interim ED?

- Would you expect compensation for being the interim ED?

- Would you consider being the interim ED for expenses only?

- Are there other ways the Board could compensate you for being the interim ED?

- Would you be willing to resign or take a leave of absence from your position on the Board to accept the interim ED position?

- Would you anticipate any problems with returning to being a Board member after being the interim ED?

- Would you be interested in being considered for the permanent ED position?

- If so, how do you think you would respond to a new ED if you were not selected for the position?

- How do you think you will be able to interact with your peers on the Board as the interim ED?

Letter of Appointment

The committee should confirm the appointment of the Board member as interim through a written memorandum or letter that specifies those areas and issues that have been agreed to by both parties. The confirmation communiqué should define the amount of compensation agreed upon, if any, and the scope of work to be done. The letter should also specify the projected time line and time commitments for the interim assignment. The letter of appointment needs to clarify who reports to the interim and to whom the interim should report. To avoid any misunderstandings, it is advisable to describe how the individual's status on the Board is to be resolved, whether it is to suspend, resign, or make some other arrangement.

An Independent Professional

An independent interim ED should be someone with extensive experience in leading nonprofit organizations, along with the expertise to assist the Board and staff to adjust to changes that will be inevitable when a new permanent ED is hired. The independent interim ED brings a professional objectivity and years of management experience that will enable a fair and comprehensive evaluation of the organization's operations.

When seeking an independent interim executive the Board should look for someone with skills and experience that will meet the needs of the organization. The Board should seek out someone with the following qualifications:

- At least five years' experience as a successful ED with a nonprofit organization.

- Specific expertise to meet the immediate challenges faced by the organization.

- Expertise in conducting institutional audits, preparing plans of correction, and implementing the plans.

- The ability to be a change agent, and the personality to implement change and accept the role of lightning rod for resistance to change.

- A working understanding of the chain of command.

- No desire to be the organization's permanent ED.

- The ability to commit to at least a four- to six-month assignment.

Hiring an independent interim will give the organization some breathing space when anticipating a lengthy search process. The combined independence and professional experience of such an individual assures an understanding of the appropriate roles and responsibilities of an interim. In many cases the organization may be able to find someone who has already served as an interim and brings a track record of success.

The independent interim can provide an objective evaluation of the organization's operations and policies and be in an excellent position to provide recommendations for change within the context of what needs to be done before and after the new ED's arrival.

The independent interim ED can also assist with the executive search process, except in the unlikely event that the individual wants to be a candidate for the permanent position.

On the downside, the Board may need to commit itself to spending time interviewing a few candidates. The cost of hiring an independent interim may be higher than that of appointing a staff or Board member. (The cost of hiring an independent interim may be equal to or exceed what the organization has budgeted for the ED's compensation package.) The Board may hire an interim who comes from a different area of the country, requiring temporary lodging. Making these arrangements takes time and requires additional costs. And an outside interim may also need time to become acquainted with the specifics of the organization's services and operations.

Additional Issues To Consider

Appointing an independent interim ED also raises a number of questions that need to be considered.

Compensation. Paying for an independent interim ED may be viewed as a disadvantage to this option, however, when put into perspective the overall cost may be well worth the investment. Retaining a seasoned professional who can quickly assume the reins of leadership will relieve the Board of many responsibilities, allowing it to address other important issues that are more within its own sphere of responsibility. When considering the cost of an independent interim ED the Board needs to calculate what is already budgeted for the ED's position. This analysis should include the budgeted amount for the following items:

- Base salary

- Cost of accrued vacation and sick leave

- Payroll taxes (FICA) paid by the organization

- Health, dental, vision, disability, unemployment, and workers compensation insurance

- The organization's contribution to the ED's Flex Plan

- The organization's contribution to the ED's retirement fund

- Other perquisites provided the ED, such as leased vehicle and housing

In general, this option may cost the organization 10 percent to 20 percent more than what is in the organization's budget for the ED's position. But if Board members are convinced that it is in the best interest of the organization, they need to find the additional resources to cover the extra cost.

For example, they might consider delaying a major program expansion or capital expenditure and using those funds to cover the additional costs of the interim. Or they might seek a special one-time grant from a long-time donor. Many funders will be responsive to such a request, when they are assured that the Board has a well-thought-out plan on how to proceed through this critical period.

References. The Board should check at least three work references from the candidate.

The Role of the Interim in the Executive Search Process. Having the independent interim ED involved in the executive search process will provide an invaluable perspective for both the Board and the candidates. The interim ED should be part of the search team, participating in the interviews and screening process. The independent's understanding of the job and the expertise needed to perform its duties is a component that will enhance the search and decision-making process.

Responsibilities and Expectations. In addition to the usual responsibilities of an interim, the independent interim ED will be able to provide the Board with the objective analysis of the organization's strengths and challenges. The individual should also be able to provide the Board with a comprehensive plan of correction that can either be started at once or held for the new ED to start the recommended changes.

Supervisory Relationships. The interim ED will interact with all members of the Board and its committee chairs. The overall supervisory line of communication should be with one member of the Board, customarily the President. The Board President and interim ED should maintain a close working relationship, which may require daily or at least weekly communication.

The interim should provide the Board President with a detailed written report on activities during the previous week. The report could also include a list of activities planned for the following week.

The interim ED usually supervises those employees who reported to the previous ED. The interim should not have the authority to hire or fire management team members without consultation and approval from the Board's Executive Committee or the full Board.

Term of Appointment. The criteria for how long to retain the services of an independent interim ED are no different from what was discussed for the other two options except that the independent interim ED has to make a firm promise to the organization to keep personal and professional obligations and schedules from interfering with the commitment to the agency.

Specific Questions to Ask Candidates for the Independent Interim ED Position. In addition to the general questions recommended earlier in this chapter, the Transition Committee should consider asking an outside candidate for interim ED these questions:

- Have you ever been an interim ED before?

- What did you enjoy about being an interim ED?

- What did you find challenging about being an interim ED?

- Why do you prefer being an interim ED to taking a permanent ED position?

- What do you know about our organization?

- What do you know about [type of nonprofit organization, such as foster care services, serving the elderly, an arts and education council, chamber of commerce]?

- Do you have the time to be a full-time interim ED?

- How long can you commit to being the interim ED?

- What compensation are you asking?

- Are there any other costs related to your being our interim ED?

- Would you be interested in being considered for the permanent ED position?

Letter of Appointment

The Board will want more than a letter of appointment when hiring an independent interim ED. The two parties should enter into a contract that outlines the roles, responsibilities, and expectations of both. The contract should include items such as these:

- Term of engagement (starting and ending dates as well as a clause that extends the contract on a month-to-month basis).

- Detailed list of expectations and role of interim.

- Clause assuring the organization that all information obtained during the interim's tenure will be held confidential.

- Indemnification of liability.

- Cancellation clause.

- Compensation agreement on base payment.

- Agreement to reimbursement of any other expenses related to the job (mileage, lodging, meals, and so on).

- Any other matters the two parties want to include.

The independent interim ED may want to be considered an independent contractor. Therefore the contract will need to be constructed in such a manner to comply with the Department of Labor's definition of an independent contractor. The Board should consult with the organization's attorney when drafting the contract.

Initial Duties

Once the interim ED has been appointed the Board President will want to announce the appointment to key stakeholder groups and individuals. This will assure stakeholders that the organization is in competent hands and that the Board is in control. The notification should go to a variety of stakeholders representing the organization's employees and volunteers, funding agencies—public and private— as well as contributors and donors, members (if a membership organization), individuals who serve on the organization's committees, and consumers of the organization's services or programs.

The interim ED will need to take care of many activities during the first few weeks on the job. The following list may help prioritize those activities and ensure that important items are not overlooked. These duties may differ depending upon the circumstances that influenced the departure of the former ED.

The following items need to be accomplished during the first few days after assuming the position of interim ED:

- Review the financial status of the organization.

    Verify balances in all bank accounts.

    Verify balance in line of credit account.

    Reconcile bank statement with checking account.

    Verify status of organization's investments.

    Review list of payables.

    Review list of receivables.

    Check receivable aging accounts.

- Meet with the management staff to review any issues about the departure of the ED and the appointment of the interim.

    Assure the staff of the interim ED's support and confidence.

    Assure the staff that their jobs are secure, if it is possible to do so. (This will reduce anxiety about that second shoe dropping.)

    Reinforce how important staff members are to the stability of the organization.

    Review all pending projects people are working on, including time lines.

    Review expectations regarding work and procedures.

    Discuss the interim ED's style of management.

    Ask if they know of any issues that may require the interim ED's immediate attention.

Set up a weekly meeting date for each individual.

Set up a time to meet the management group on at least a monthly basis.

- Meet with all members of the Board's Executive Committee to obtain an understanding of their concerns, needs, and strengths.

Review their understanding of the roles and responsibilities of the Board.

Discuss their expectations during the transition period.

Compile a list of what must be accomplished during the next four to six months.

Determine how best to communicate with them (by phone, e-mail, or fax).

Establish a basic understanding of the chain of command.

Obtain information about the style of meetings and their level of formality; review agendas from previous meetings.

Determine role of interim ED when attending Board and committee meetings. Is the interim ED expected to make reports at these meetings, take minutes, develop agendas?

Besides all the tasks outlined in the preceding list, at some point in the process, the interim ED should also do the following:

- Meet with the departing ED if the Board deems it appropriate.

Review pending projects that will need follow-up.

Discuss management styles, both similarities and differences.

Obtain insights on any issues related to existing staff.

The interim will want to meet with key stakeholder groups to gain insight into the relationships among the various stakeholders. Having the interim ED visible within the community assures everyone that the organization is in good hands, providing a sense of stability and confidence in the organization's future.

To assist the interim ED in establishing authority, Board members must clearly state their full support and confidence in the interim ED's ability to all stakeholders. One way to demonstrate their commitment to the executive transition process—and the interim ED's status—is to agree to retain the interim ED for estimated time it will take to make structural or systemic changes as identified as needing to be corrected before the new ED is hired, or for the projected time for recruiting, screening, and hiring a permanent ED.

The interim ED and the Board leadership need to communicate with each other quite frequently. This will help both parties avoid any surprises and will strengthen the level of shared leadership that must be developed.

The interim also needs to establish a sense of loyalty with the staff and enforce the basic understanding that the rules of order are still in effect. The organization's standard operating procedures for grievances should be maintained and enforced. No member of the staff should be allowed to contact a member of the Board with a complaint or comment about the interim's performance outside the established protocol. If the Board permits deviation from the established process, it runs the risk that both the involved Board members and the employee will continue such behavior when the new ED arrives.

The interim ED may experience resistance to change and should be skilled in knowing how to respond to such resistance. Having the interim ED deal with the resistance may help reduce the level of opposition to changes that will inevitably be implemented by the permanent ED when the transition is complete.

The circumstances affecting the departure of the ED will be a good indicator of the probability of encountering staff members with strong feelings of anger or fear. If the Board decided that a change in leadership was needed, the staff members who have worked with the departing ED may feel the decision was unwarranted and unfair. The reaction from the staff will need to be addressed. The interim ED should help staff members express their feelings and bring closure to the situation. The interim's focus should be to get the staff in the right frame of mind to accept the new ED with excitement and loyalty.

The interim should be prepared to be the target of the staff's feelings about the transition. Staff members may see the interim as the cause or at least the representative of those who caused their friend, mentor, and protector to depart. They may even try to undermine the newcomer's work or credibility. These efforts may be demonstrated through blatant or passive-aggressive behaviors. The interim ED is responsible for helping staff members successfully resolve their feelings so they can be ready for the hiring of the next ED. If the ED's departure was due to the Sudden Loss Factor, the interim will need to work with the staff and Board as they go through the natural grieving process. This may result in the inability to focus on the tasks at hand. Patience, support, and understanding are all qualities an interim may need to display in this circumstance.

If the departure was something that both Board and staff felt was long overdue, the interim will have an environment in which everyone should be ready to plan and implement change. This gives the interim ED the opportunity to provide the essential guidance to ensure both Board and staff work together following a defined planning process. All too often when stakeholders have been waiting a long time to begin the planning journey, they tend to move too quickly, which may result in a plan that addresses immediate issues but does not provide long-term direction. In other words, the focus may be on operational issues to the exclusion of essential strategic decisions and policies.

Dealing with Organizational Problems

In the course of the job, the interim ED may discover problems involving issues such as these:

- *Financial difficulties:* The agency may have cash-flow problems, unpaid or late payments of state or federal employee withholding taxes, aging payables of sixty days or longer, a checking account below the bank's minimum requirements, or a maximized line of credit. It may have budget problems reflected in its profit-and-loss reports. An analysis of the various cost centers and how the administrative costs are determined and then allocated to each cost center may be needed. A review of past audits and the accompanying management letters may also provide insights into the financial issues facing the organization and the interim Executive Director.

- *Personnel problems:* There may be problem areas in the agency's personnel policies and procedures, organizational issues related to work flow or lines of communication, under- or overstaffing, excess sick or personnel leave time. The issues may include insufficient or inconsistent salary administration. Outdated job descriptions and job performance evaluations may also need attention. Problems may also be manifested by complaints of sexual harassment or unfair treatment under the Americans with Disabilities Act (ADA).

- *Accountability issues:* The agency may not be fulfilling requirements of specific grants or other restricted funding.

- *Administrative issues:* There may be a lack of management systems, written operating procedures, or strategic and operational goals.

- *Governance issues:* Committees may be inactive or ineffective, and Board members may not understand their roles and responsibilities. The Board may lack diversity of thought, skills, or demographics.

- *Corporate culture difficulties:* The agency may suffer from low morale, poor teamwork, and absence of a sense of urgency and consensus building. The organization may need to strengthen its enthusiasm, trust, and focus on consumer services, and its entrepreneurial, risk-taking spirit.

In dealing with these and other issues, an interim ED can be pivotal in paving the way for the new Executive Director. In Chapter Three we mentioned an organization that was taking the Ostrich Approach until it was told by its funding source that its ED was not meeting expectations. The Board retained the services of an independent interim ED who quickly identified numerous operational inefficiencies. The organizational culture left much to be desired. Internal mistrust and animosity on the part of the staff were so ingrained that reorganization with the elimination of specific positions was the obvious first step in changing the organization's operations. Upon bringing his evaluation of the challenges to the Board and making specific recommendations, the interim was authorized to begin taking action to correct the situation, before a new ED was to be hired. After a year with the new ED, the organization is now a model of how change can work—as described by the funder that had threatened to pull its support.

By the time the new ED was retained the staff had been restructured and downsized. New personnel policies had been drafted and were in the process of being reviewed and approved by the Board. The reorganization was on its way. The new ED was able to hire a new management team and take charge of the organization's operation.

In conclusion, the placement of an interim ED is a decision that requires the Board to consider the organization's immediate needs and how the options discussed in this chapter can best meet those needs. The selection of the interim ED is not just to get a warm body in there to hold down the fort. The "warm body" may not be the best solution in preparing the organization for its new ED. The appointment of a professional independent interim may be the best investment the Board could make at this critically important crossroads.

6

Recruiting and Screening the New Executive Director

Once it has decided which option to pursue in seeking an interim ED, the Board needs to turn its attention to the process of deciding when, how, and where to search for a new permanent ED. The most important decision a nonprofit Board makes is the selection of a new professional leader, the ED. As with other steps in the transition, the search should begin with a plan—and what kind of plan it is depends on why the ED left in the first place.

Transition Types

The organization may be faced with any of four types of transitions:

- *Following the Leader:* Adjusting to the departure of a long-term ED or someone who started the agency will be difficult for the Board, staff, funders, consumers, and other key stakeholders. The next ED will need to be skilled in helping everyone associated with the organization adjust to the absence of a respected and valued leader. Many who attempt to replace a founder or longtime ED do not succeed. This is usually because the Board and agency did not take the time to prepare for and understand the inevitable differences between the previous ED and the new one.

- *Hanging by Their Fingernails:* The agency may face problems with finances, programs, personnel, governance, or overall management. These problems may have been what caused the ED to

BE PREPARED TO MAKE DIFFICULT DECISIONS

leave (the Burnout or Cutting the Mustard Factors). It will take an experienced administrator and manager to lead the organization through the identification of the issues and the problem-solving process. Simple survival will depend on finding a new ED with the leadership and administrative abilities to turn the organization from its present disastrous course.

• *Running in Place:* This refers to an agency that has been providing the same services for a long time, and although those services may have been adequate when they were created, the organization has not been responsive to changing community needs. The agency is underachieving and is now perceived as unable to meet the present needs of its clients. The next ED will need to help the Board and staff consider various options for restoring growth to the organization. The new ED must be visionary, creative, and able to be a change leader. The individual must have the motivational and communication skills to keep the Board, staff, funders, and others on the prescribed course.

• *At the Starting Block:* The agency is about to hire its first paid ED. This ED will need to help the Board adjust to giving up its involvement with day-to-day operations. The new ED will need to be experienced in establishing agency management procedures and will need the skills to work with the Board and other volunteers and staff who have been responsible for the organization's success. This transition period requires patience and diplomacy. The new ED will need to be a communicator, self-starter, and someone with good follow-up skills. Most start-up organizations are usually understaffed, so the ED will need to be able to manage and organize multiple tasks.

Identify Immediate and Future Issues

Before the discussion of recruiting and retaining a new ED begins, the Board needs to know what critical issues will be confronting the organization in the near and distant future. The Board should identify emerging industry trends and issues and their possible impact on the organization—and on its vision—before considering what type of staff leadership will be needed.

This process is usually accomplished at a Board retreat with the assistance of a skilled facilitator. Key management staff should be included. As discussed earlier, this process is not strategic planning, it is an exercise of reviewing, verifying, and if appropriate revising the Board's previous work on its vision for the future.

Consider a Merger

Before proceeding with the next two steps it is advisable to stop and consider a question that is often overlooked when in the executive transition mode: "Is this the opportune time to consider seeking a merger or some other form of strategic partnership with another organization?" Considering such a move will depend on what issues face the organization and its capacity to address them.

Many challenges confront the nonprofit industry. One of them is the vast proliferation of nonprofit organizations. The competition for funding and manpower (staff and volunteers) is a continual challenge for many organizations.

Thomas A. McLaughlin, in *Nonprofit Mergers and Alliances* (1998), puts it this way: "Having an excessive number of nonprofit organizations actually weakens the collective power of the entire field. Organizations that should be serving a mission must instead spend disproportionate amounts of resources worrying about how they are going to fund it, manage it, and perpetuate it." McLaughlin goes on to predict that the new focus of strategic planning in the nonprofit sector will be the consideration of alliances.

A merger is easier to consider and implement when one of the partners is without an ED. The absence of an ED removes the potential minefield of a power struggle between two strong staff leaders.

When considering this option, the Board may want to look for a management transition company to help identify potential partners, conduct a due diligence process, and negotiate the conditions of the merger.

Dick was invited to meet with a small organization that had a budget of less than $300,000 and only two full-time staff in addition to the ED. The very dedicated Board members were burned out and frustrated because they had just lost their third ED in six years. They were discussing an executive search process when Dick raised the option of seeking a partner for a strategic alliance. The Board recognized that raising the $300,000 every year over the next five to ten years would be a monumental task in the face of competition from other agencies, and that turnover in the ED's position would be a chronic challenge, considering the issues and pressures this small organization faced.

So the Board took advantage of the void in the ED's position to authorize a search for compatible organizations interested in a partnership. The organization was still financially sound and therefore able to initiate the search for a partner on its own terms. Within three months it had partnered with a larger, more established organization whose mission and values were essentially the same as its own. The organization's services continue today; three members of its Board are now also members of the partner's Board, and its long-respected reputation continues to attract donors.

Define What Will Be Expected from the New ED

If the Board decides not to initiate a search for a strategic partner, it should move forward with preparing and implementing the executive search process.

To start with, it should survey the Board members requesting they indicate, in priority order, what they will be expecting from the new ED. The survey should also request a listing, again in priority order, of what skills and qualities the new ED should possess. Use these lists to adapt the existing ED job description to the current needs. Both the lists and the new job description will keep the search on target, will give prospective candidates a better picture of the position and of the Board's expectations, and will provide the basic format to use when developing a rating system for the interview process.

It is important that the Board be cautious when developing these lists. They should not set out to describe the skills or qualities held by the beloved and respected ED whose services they have lost or are about to lose. *Cloning has yet to be perfected!* Nor should they develop the list with the negative aspects of the last ED in mind. They must focus on fulfilling the organization's vision. The Board's responses will establish the criteria for recruitment and screening.

Develop Strategies for Recruiting the Next ED

When the Board has identified what it will take to move the organization toward its vision, it will need to turn its attention to finding the best individual for the job, someone who demonstrates abilities, expertise, and experience that offer the greatest chance of meeting the expectations expressed by the Board.

The first option is to look within the organization for the next ED. Hiring someone already familiar with the organization is not only commendable but also prudent. It is usually good policy to give staff members opportunities for advancement. If the organization has been grooming someone internally as heir apparent, the decision about the next ED should be easy.

But before appointing a successor from within the organization, consider this: If the internal audits and Board assessments have identified organizational and systemic problems, it is important to be sure that the individual being considered was not part of the problem and is in fact capable of breaking away from the old regime and making the changes needed. If there are any questions or concerns about the individual, the Board should move forward with the search process.

If the Board decides to go outside the organization to look for its new ED, it is perfectly natural to look at EDs of other organizations. In fact, Board members should always be cognizant of EDs of other organizations—even before an ED announces a decision to leave. Reaching out to other leaders when faced with the loss of one's own Executive Director is not an unusual or unethical event. Executive search firms use this technique quite successfully. Organizations faced with an ED transition will naturally seek to recruit an individual who has a proven track record and, preferably, is known to one or more of the Board members. Being on the other end of the Godfather Factor is not bad.

Other Issues

Before progressing too far into the search process the Board will need to establish a compensation package for the ED's position. This includes the salary range and list of benefits. In addition, the Board will need to decide whether to offer the new ED relocation costs, if needed. If so, it will have to consider whether to put a cap on those costs or to pay whatever it takes.

The Board will also need to consider whether the new ED should be offered a contract or employment under an "at will" arrangement with a letter of appointment. Whichever is offered, the new ED should be eligible for all benefits covered in the organization's personnel policies and procedures that apply to all employees. Special arrangements (such as paying the premium for family health insurance or allowing more sick and vacation days than provided other staff) above the personnel policies should be covered in the contract or letter of appointment.

Have a Backup Plan

What will the Board do if the organization goes through the search and interview processes and the first choice turns down the job offer? How far down the list of candidates should the Board go before stopping and starting all over again? Although this scenario occurs rarely, it is always a good idea to have a contingency plan for the unexpected.

We recommend that the Board consider offering the position to the next-best candidate only if the vast majority of the Board members are comfortable with that option and the reasons this candidate wasn't the first choice didn't include issues of trust or competency. The Board needs to take its time when reconsidering this candidate. It may even be helpful to ask the individual to return for another interview.

If there is no real second choice, don't force the offer on someone willy-nilly. We have seen a few instances where a Board even went down to the third choice and regretted it within a few months after the new ED had been on the job.

When faced with the challenge of not finding a fit the first time, try again. Before reembarking on the search process, however, the Transition Committee needs to objectively evaluate why the original process did not produce a candidate that was willing to accept the position and acceptable to the Board.

Candidates usually reject an offer for one or more of the following reasons:

- The job description did not adequately portray the organization's needs.

- The compensation package was not fully discussed at some point in the interview process. (We recommend that it be discussed during the first few interviews.)

- The candidate did not feel comfortable with the organization's culture, leadership, or mission. They just did not feel there was a good fit from their perspective.

The Board's reasons for not selecting any of the candidates often boil down to not feeling there was a good fit. Another reason is that the Board's expectations and perceptions of the needed skill sets were not communicated fully. Sometimes the committee has accepted the need for a different type of ED from the previous incumbent and the Board is still looking for a clone.

Whatever the reasons, they must be identified and resolved before going forward with a second search process. This may also be the time when the Board and Transition Committee need to reconsider using a search company.

Transition and Post-Transition Considerations

When an ED announces a plan to leave the organization, a number of questions need to be addressed:

- Will the departure occur before a new ED can be recruited and hired? If so, then an interim ED may be necessary.

- Can the departure be delayed until the new ED has been found?

- If the ED delays departure until the new ED is hired, how long should the organization plan for a reasonable overlap?

The departing ED's participation in orienting the new ED can only be considered if the departure of the ED is of a positive nature—the Godfather Factor (being offered a better position) or the Gone Fishing Factor (retirement). An ED who is leaving because of the Burnout Factor may not offer the new ED the best introduction to the position or the organization. After all, how useful would those three envelopes really be? Needless to say, if the ED's departure is due to the Cutting the Mustard Factor, any involvement in the orientation of the new ED would be inappropriate.

Some Boards worry that without a lengthy overlap the new ED's orientation will not be successful and the transition will not be smooth. It can be tempting to try to get the ED to stay longer than the traditional thirty-day notice period.

What is an appropriate time for an overlap? There is no set rule, since each situation is different, but a few considerations can help establish an appropriate time frame for the departing ED to stay on and provide guidance and orientation to the new ED.

Clearly identify those areas in the orientation for the new ED that will need to be provided by the departing ED. The best role the departing ED can play in the orientation process is assisting in reviewing specific personnel and governance issues facing the organization. Ask the departing ED to share information and observations about matters related to personnel policies and procedures and how the Board functions.

The departing ED will be an invaluable asset when it comes to introducing the new ED to key stakeholders of the organization. The departing ED's relationships with funders, contributors, consumers of the organization's services and programs, and public policymakers have been cultivated over the years. The new ED will need to establish such relationships, and having the departing ED open the door for the initial contact may be helpful.

At the same time, bear in mind that a new ED who is an experienced leader and administrator may need only minimal orientation to the organization's administrative functions and services. The new ED will also have sources of information other than the departing ED, including Board members and other officers of the organization. And the secretary or administrative assistant assigned to the new ED will usually be the most valued member of the orientation team, being (if the organization runs true to type) invariably the best-informed person on the staff.

The overlap period may be driven by specific factors affecting the organization. For example, it may be involved in a major capital fundraising campaign or a major retooling of its information technology. Keeping the departing ED on board to complete a special project may be a prudent decision, assuming the individual retains the trust of the organization.

The Board should be cautious when the departing ED advocates a long overlap. The recommendation may be a result of cold feet—the inability to move on to other opportunities—or to an inflated estimation of the ED's own influence and importance.

Having a long overlap period may be beneficial, but it also may cause a lot of problems for the new ED, especially if the departing ED's presence is so powerful that it impedes the smooth transition from one leader to another.

The length of time of the overlap should be specific to the needs of the organization. As a general rule of thumb, however, it should be kept as short as possible and clearly defined before the new ED is hired. The new ED needs to know what is in store before accepting the position (*no surprises* and *full disclosure*). In addition, the new ED should be able to request that the overlap be reduced or ended if it is no longer needed or if it is inhibiting the new ED's ability to become established in the job.

Regardless of the length of the overlap, it is tempting to offer a departing ED who is leaving in a blaze of glory either a Board seat or a consulting role. *Avoid this*. It is very difficult to make changes and to transfer power and leadership when the former director is in the room. We have seen numerous occasions when the break was not clean and the new ED was tempted to go screaming into the night.

Recruitment and Screening

Boards often underestimate the time needed to deal with the complexities and legalities related to the executive search. It needs a working knowledge of federal and sometimes state laws such as these:

- Title VII of the Civil Rights Act of 1964

- The Americans with Disabilities Act of 1990

- The Age Discrimination Act of 1967

- The Equal Pay Act of 1963

- Sections 503 and 504 of the Rehabilitation Act of 1974

This is a time when the help of a human resource professional or an attorney who works in the area of employment rights can be very beneficial. In addition, we recommend that the Board verify that its Directors and Officers insurance has employment practices liability coverage. This is very important: Don't behave like Scarlet O'Hara and wait for tomorrow. The coverage will not prevent a miscue or a poorly worded interview question, but it should cover the cost of a defense against a lawsuit and may even pay a penalty if one is awarded.

Conducting a search will take a commitment of more than a hundred workhours over three to four months, perhaps much more. How can it take so long? A well-placed announcement of the position could result in fifty to more than a hundred résumés. It usually takes ten to fifteen minutes to review and rate each résumé, so reviewing a hundred résumés will take approximately twenty to twenty-five hours, just to decide which candidates to interview. And still more time will have to go into conducting the visioning review process and surveying the Board for its expectations, revising the job description, doing the research necessary to develop a competitive compensation package, composing the announcement of the job opening, developing the questions that will be asked at the various interviews, checking references, and scheduling interviews and meetings. Then the interviews themselves will absorb many hours of the Board's time.

We have seen too many Boards embark on the recruiting process and then run into problems with meeting established time lines. The Board may initially attempt to meet the time demands of the search, but family and personal work requirements may conflict with the search needs. The Board volunteers may find that the process is taking longer than originally projected, which compounds the challenge of attracting qualified candidates.

Not staying on task and meeting established time lines may cause a number of problems. Qualified candidates who are interested may not be able to wait for the Board to make a decision. And candidates who are highly sought after may encounter the Godfather Factor and get an offer they can't refuse from another organization.

Once the process starts, it should proceed on task within the established time lines. If nothing else, if it takes too long, it may convey a perception that the organization is disorganized or leaderless at the Board level, and many qualified candidates may reconsider their interest once they get that idea.

If the time commitment is too great—and if the Board lacks the expertise—it may decide not conduct the search itself. If that is the case, the Board has two other options. It can appoint a Search Committee made up of both Board members and others from the community, or it can seek the services of an executive search firm.

Search Committee

It is hard for the full Board to conduct a well-organized executive search. We recommend the appointment of a Search Committee of five to seven members. Some of the Board's leadership should be on the committee, especially the President and Vice President, assuming there is a progression policy where the VP will become President in a year or two. Other members of the committee could be individuals who have experience in human resources and conducting searches for professional positions.

The Search Committee should develop a proposed budget for the search process to be presented to the Board for approval.

It should include the following items:

- *Advertising:* This may include the cost of posting job announcements in local and other city newspapers, in professional and trade publications, and on the Web, as well as printing flyers to be sent to various service and professional organizations.

- *Long distance phone calls and faxes:* These may be necessary to talk with candidates and their references.

- *Travel:* If any of the final candidates live out of town, the organization may want to offer to cover the cost of travel, lodging, and meals for those asked to return for the final round of interviews.

- *Relocation costs:* The Board may include as part of the negotiated compensation package payment for all or part of moving expenses for the new ED if that individual lives out of town.

Committee members can conduct the search themselves, or they may want to consider the hiring of a search firm to assist them. If that is the option they choose, then the cost of the search firm should be included in the budget as another line item.

Executive Search Service

Using an outside search company provides the Search Committee (or the full Board, if that's where the decision is made) with the needed expertise to ensure that the process will be conducted in a timely and efficient manner. Using a search firm changes the role of the Board or Search Committee to some extent, although the hiring of a search firm does not mean that the organization's representatives abdicate their participation in the process or responsibility of making the hiring decision.

The tasks delegated to the search firm include the initial search and screening, within the parameters of the job description and based on the expectations, skills, and qualities identified by the Board. It is imperative that the company hired to conduct the search be thoroughly acquainted with the organization, its vision for the future, and the challenges it faces. The partnership between the Board or committee and the person conducting the search must be based on trust and respect. A successful search process cannot be accomplished if information about the organization is withheld. The search firm expects *no surprises*. The committee needs to share information about the organization with full disclosure as a guiding principle.

To protect the organization from inappropriate disclosures of proprietary information, the contract between the two parties should include a confidentiality clause. This will clarify the expectation that the search firm is not to divulge any sensitive personnel, program, and financial information about the organization during or after the search process. We have provided a sample contract between an organization and a search firm as Resource A at the end of the book. The organization's attorney should review any contract to make sure it is protecting its interests.

The organization should expect the search firm to provide the following basic services:

- Plan and implement the overall process.

- Facilitate the visioning process with the Board.

- Conduct and analyze the survey of the Board members.

- Review and rewrite job description based on Board's expectations.

- Help define compensation package that is competitive for the marketplace.

- Create and place all job announcements.

- Use its network in the nonprofit and business community to locate individuals who may be excellent candidates or may know of potential candidates.

- Review and rate all résumés.

- Conduct interviews and check references with the top candidates.

- Facilitate the interview process between the committee and the top candidates.

- Facilitate the interview process between the top candidates selected by the committee and the full Board.

- Assist the Board with negotiations with the final candidate.

The search firm may also offer other activities. For example, some search firms will maintain contact with the Board and new ED to provide assistance during the first twelve months, in the event the Board and the new ED run into problems with the transition process. Some firms will offer to provide workshops on Board and staff relationships and change management at no additional cost or at a much-reduced rate.

The executive search firm may offer a guarantee, which usually relates to how long the new ED will stay with the organization. For example, the guarantee may commit the firm to conduct the search all over again if the new ED is terminated or departs for job-related reasons within the first twelve months. Having a guarantee gives the Board some protection from a bad hire. The guarantee may have some contingencies that the organization will need to agree to. Read these carefully and be sure your organization can fulfill these requirements. We have provided a sample of a guarantee as Resource B at the end of the book. Once again the organization's attorney should review the guarantee to ensure it is in the best interest of the organization.

If the committee decides to seek an outside executive search service, it will want to be sure the company is a good fit with the organization and its needs. The organization can issue a Request for Proposals. That will require a review and interview process with respondents. The Search Committee should be authorized to conduct a search for the search firm. Whether the RFP has been issued or the Search Committee invites specific firms to submit proposals, the committee will want to interview a potential search firm. The following questions are useful to ask when choosing an executive search firm:

- What search and selection process will be used, and what is the role of the organization's Board and committee in that process?

- What is the fee? Does it include all out-of-pocket expenses? If not, what is the estimate of those costs and what does it cover?

- What is the estimated time line for finding the final candidates for Board review? Is it more than four months? If so, why?

- How many final candidates will be brought to the Board for consideration? If it's less than three, why?

- What happens if the final three candidates introduced to the Board for review all turn down the position, or the Board does not offer the position to any of them? Will the search continue at no cost? If not, what will be the cost?

- Will the company assist the Board in negotiating an agreement with the final candidate? Will the company provide the Board with information about a competitive compensation package (salary and benefits)?

- Is a guarantee offered? If so, what is it? What length of time does it cover? Are there any exceptions that would invalidate the guarantee? Are there any conditions that have to be met by the Board in order to maintain the guarantee?

- Are there any value-added bonuses that go with the contract? If so, what are they?

The cost of an executive search is rarely in the organization's annual budget. It may be difficult to cover the cost of a comprehensive search process that includes a search firm. The Board may need to consider accessing its reserves or appealing to one or two of its long-time investors for the funds. This is not the time for the Board to try to find ways to shortcut the process because funds are limited. The wrong hire will be much more costly in the long term. Some search firms base their fee on a percentage (usually 20 percent to 30 percent) of the compensation to be provided the new ED, others charge a fixed fee. Whichever method is used, the fee may or may not include out-of-pocket costs related to the search, such as advertising, long-distance calls, and travel. As noted in the question list, it's essential to clarify what is and what is not included in the fee.

The Search Process

Regardless of whether the Search Committee or an executive search firm conducts the search, the following sequence of events should be followed:

1. Review and confirm expectations of the new ED; revise the job description and compensation package as needed.
2. Announce position availability.
3. Review and rate all résumés.
4. Interview and screen candidates.
   a. Conduct preliminary interviews with top applicants.
   b. Check references.
   c. Conduct detailed interviews with finalists.
   d. Offer position and negotiate agreement.

Announce Position Availability

The development of the announcement should be assigned to someone who is familiar with placing job announcements. The cost of placing an advertisement in a newspaper depends on its length, so be concise but informative, use abbreviations, and include only those items that are absolutely necessary to attract qualified candidates.

The scope of the search needs to be defined. Should it be limited to the local area, or should it be expanded to a state, regional, national, or even an international search? If the search can encompass a wide geographic area, the announcement may be placed in professional and trade publications and on Internet sites. These outlets may permit a more detailed description of the job, which could include the list of expectations, skills, and qualifications needed. Before submitting the announcement, be sure to check the cost.

When using a search firm the committee members need to decide if they want to review all material before it is released to the public or permit the announcements to go out without an approval process. The committee needs to be able to trust the search firm to have the expertise to draft and place job announcements without committee oversight. The search firm should also have information about individuals in the business and nonprofit community who meet or exceed the job's criteria and may be interested in applying for the position.

Review and Rate All Résumés

Generally a well-constructed and strategically placed job announcement will generate a large number of résumés and applications—especially in a very competitive economy, where exciting, challenging opportunities do not often present themselves. Each résumé will require a review and rating based on the established criteria and qualifications set by the Board. In addition, we have found ourselves looking at other factors that also influence our rating of the candidate's suitability for the position:

- Spelling errors, typographical errors, and poor grammar
- Lack of information about the candidate's accomplishments
- Important dates inaccurate or missing
- Poor formatting and excessive length
- Contact information inaccurate or missing

Surprising as it seems, we often come across résumés of potential candidates who can't be reached because the contact information they have provided is either wrong or incomplete—assuming they've provided any at all. In addition, we often see résumés from individuals who are completely unqualified. It is amazing how many individuals with minimal management experience believe they could serve as Executive Director of a nonprofit organization, and pay no attention to the announced criteria. Unfortunately all these résumés take time to review.

Exhibit 6.1 is a sample of a rating form that could be used with résumés.

Interview and Screen Candidates

Once all of the résumés have been reviewed and rated, the process should produce at least eight to ten candidates who meet or exceed expectations. At this point the search enters the interviewing and screening phase. We have found that it usually takes a number of interviews with the candidates before a decision can be reached. These interviews tend to fall into several types:

- Initial interview via a telephone conversation

- Preliminary individual face-to-face interview, conducted by the search firm

- Interviews with the Search Committee, followed by an interview with the Board

The search firm in consultation with the Search Committee may recommend additional interviews with the management team and interviews with representatives of stakeholder groups, such as an advisory council, users of the organization's services or programs, key funding groups, and strategic alliance partners. These groups may also be involved if it is believed that they will add information that will help with the final decision or because they will be an important part

Exhibit 6.1. Résumé Rating Form

Rate the candidate for the listed categories as follows: 3 = exceeds expectations; 2 = meets expectations; 1 = does not meet expectations.

Résumé	Five to Ten Years' Experience in High Management Position	Experience with Nonprofit Organizations and Boards of Directors	Working Understanding of the Agency's Field	Experience with Agency's Consumer Population	Experience with Operating Budgets	Demonstrated Leadership Ability	Résumé Well Constructed and Prepared	Total Points
# 1								
# 2								
# 3								
# 4								
# 5								
. . .								

of the transition process after the new ED is on the job. Giving them an opportunity to provide their perceptions of the candidates may enhance their support of the final decision.

For example, we recommend that the key management staff be involved in the screening process, meeting with the top two or three candidates before the Board does. It should be made clear that the candidates are interviewing the staff rather than the reverse, but it is acceptable for staff to be given an opportunity to share their impressions with the Search Committee. The staff should be counseled that although their involvement is important and the Search Committee and Board will want to hear their input, the final decision and responsibility remain with the Board.

At the end of each interview and screening phase, the list of candidates will most likely be reduced, until the process gets to the final interviews, first with the Search Committee and then with the full Board when the remaining two or three candidates are presented.

General Interviewing Guidelines

Interviewing a candidate is a very serious process. As we pointed out earlier, a number of legalities must be followed to protect the rights of candidates. Asking the wrong question can create a significant legal problem resulting in a financial penalty. We recommend that the Board take two steps to protect itself. First, be sure that the individual or group facilitating the interview process is experienced in structuring questions, and second, provide a detailed orientation to the process and the importance of staying with the prepared questions. If a search firm is involved it can perform that service.

Interviewing a candidate is usually the primary way the searchers are going to be able to observe the candidate's ability to relate to others, solve problems on the fly, evaluate personal strengths and limitations, and communicate successfully.

One of the most important results of the series of interviews will be the level of comfort the searchers develop with the candidate.

We advise our clients that all the candidates who pass the initial screening will almost certainly have the experience, expertise, and professional qualifications and abilities to perform the job. The real criterion that will eventually be the decision maker will be the chemistry the Board members feel exists between them and the candidate. We counsel our clients who may be struggling with a decision between two highly qualified candidates to consider their comfort level with each candidate.

It is important to remember that an interview is not a casual conversation with little or no structure. Preparation on the part of the interviewer is very important. The individual or group participating in the interviews should have a well-prepared list of questions ready to be asked of all candidates. The process needs to be designed to be as fair as possible, allowing all candidates to be playing on a level field. The interviewers should be comparing each candidate on an equal basis to an external standard. Therefore, *the same questions should be asked of all candidates*, though the interviewer should feel free to deviate from the prepared questions when more information is needed. Follow-up questions are fine, such as: "Could you expand more on what you meant by [some statement]?" or "I'm interested in hearing more about how you handled that situation. Could you expand your response?"

We have found that assigning a question to each participant keeps everyone involved and allows the candidate to interact with each member of the interviewing group.

The interviewer should assume that most if not all candidates have prepared for the interview. Therefore, the standard questions— "Will you tell me about yourself?" and the like—will probably get a well-rehearsed response. Instead, the interviewer should structure the questions to cover accomplishments at past workplaces, following up to test the candidate's ability to learn from mistakes with a question such as, "What are you disappointed with from past work experiences, and what did you learn from these situations?" This will provide the interviewer with the opportunity to see what the candidate thinks is important. It's also a measure of how well the candidate can organize thoughts on an unprepared topic.

Interview questions should focus on the candidate's experiences that are relevant to the ED's position. The examples used in the preceding paragraph are experiential. Other questions should also be focused on hypothetical situations relating to challenges that may be faced by a new ED. For example: "Our organization needs to put more emphasis on fundraising efforts. How would you go about helping us meet that goal?" This requires the candidate to demonstrate understanding of how to organize a fundraising effort. Situational questions are always a good way to see how well the candidate is informed on an area of organizational interest.

One technique that we have found helpful is to develop a situational scenario with related questions and send it to the candidates. The request could be that they prepare a five- or ten-minute verbal response or ask that they send their written response prior to the interview and be prepared to discuss it on the spot. This permits the interviewer to evaluate the candidates' written skills and their ability to verbally defend their written positions. Here is an example of a scenario provided to one of our clients prior to the interviews with the search committee.

> One of the concerns raised in our last annual financial audit related to the way undesignated funds were being distributed to the various program services and how management costs were being appropriated.
>
> Please write your response to the following questions and send them to our offices within the next five days.
>
> - How would you go about addressing the issue of allocating unrestricted funds to our various program services?
>
> - How would you approach allocating management costs to program service budgets?
>
> - What are your expectations from an annual audit and its management letter?

As indicated earlier, you should expect that each candidate has prepared for the interview. We are often more inclined to give candidates higher ratings if they demonstrate they have taken the time to get to know the organization, the field in which the organization operates, and the community the organization serves. It is very obvious which candidates have prepared and which have not.

Each phase of the interview process will have its own goals, so the focus of the interview and questions will be somewhat different as the candidate meets with the various interviewing groups.

Telephone Interviews

After the résumés have been reviewed and rated, the top seven to ten candidates should be scheduled for an initial screening interview via telephone. (Using the telephone for this round saves time and lets you have the first interview with the candidate on a relatively informal basis.)

The first objective in the phone interview is to determine how much the candidate knows about the organization. If the advertisement for the position was a "blind ad" that did not identify the organization, or if the individual is not familiar with the organization, it will be necessary to briefly describe the agency, using a short but informative description of the organization prepared before the phone calls are initiated. The interviewer should use that resource as the reference point when describing the organization to each candidate, or assessing how well the candidate has researched the organization and its needs. A well-prepared description will ensure consistency in the process.

Regardless of who describes the organization, the candidate or the interviewer, the next step is to find out if there is a reasonable fit between the candidate's job and compensation expectations and the organization's expectations and compensation ranges. Questions early in the interview should include what the candidate considers a fair starting salary and benefits package (health, life, disability, dental, and vision insurance; retirement; vehicle allowance). If the candidate's expectations exceed the established salary range or benefit package, it may be best to terminate the interview rather than waste everyone's time.

However, if the candidate is asking more than the organization can give, do some additional probing before stopping the process. The candidate's first response is not necessarily a final position. Be careful not to enter into negotiations, but attempt to determine if the candidate is amenable to discussing a range that both parties could work within if an offer were to be made. Declaring the Board's established range should either encourage the candidate to consider continuing interest in the position or to decide that it is not worth moving forward with the process.

Assuming there's some basis for further interaction, review the search process and determine dates and times the candidate may be available if invited to participate in the next screening phase. As a by-product of these discussions, the interviewer can develop a sense of the candidate's ability to relate to someone over the phone.

The following questions may also be used in the telephone interview:

- What would you consider your greatest strength as a leader?

- What skill sets do you possess that qualify you as a strong candidate for the position of Executive Director of an organization such as [name of organization]?

- What are you doing currently?

- What are your responsibilities in your present job?

- What do you like most about your present job?

- What frustrates you most about your present job?

- What questions do you have about [name of organization]?

Other questions related to the organization's needs, such as fund-raising and capital campaigns, could be substituted or added to this list. Construct such questions in very preliminary terms, however. Remember this may be only the first of a series of interviews with this candidate.

The interviewer may at this point be able to determine if the candidate will be invited to continue the process. If so, be sure that the candidate understands that the process will entail a variety of different interview opportunities with various groups and at different times. If not, end the conversation with a thank-you for the person's interest in the position. Advise all candidates that they will be notified of the results of the interview in a few days.

It is good public relations for the organization to send a letter to all candidates interviewed, thanking them for their participation and their interest in the position. Those candidates not being invited to continue should be informed of that fact and wished good fortune in their job search. Those candidates being invited to participate in a face-to-face interview should have the invitation confirmed, restating the date, time, and place of the interview. Include the name and phone number of a contact person in case a question or problem occurs.

The candidates should be asked to send a fax or e-mail message with the names, addresses, and phone numbers of three *work* references, if they were not included with the résumé.

Exhibit 6.2 is a sample of a rating form that could be used with telephone interviews.

The In-Person Interview

Once the first list of candidates is reduced as a result of the telephone interviews, the remaining candidates are invited to participate in face-to-face interviews with the Search Committee or search consultant. If possible these interviews should be conducted at the offices of the organization. The offices should provide a business environment that conveys the importance and seriousness of the interviews.

In the case of candidates who live in another city, the interviews could be conducted using teleconferencing facilities. The organization may be able to find a benefactor with teleconference facilities

Exhibit 6.2.   Sample Phone Interview Worksheet

1. Candidate's stated salary expectations: $_____
2. Expected Benefits:
   - Health Insurance
   - Coverage for Family
   - Dental Insurance
   - Vision Insurance
   - Life Insurance
   - Disability Insurance
   - Retirement
   - Vehicle Allowance
   - Moving Allowance
   - Educational Opportunities
   - Professional Conference Attendance
3. Strengths listed:
4. Special skill sets listed (fundraising, special events, arts, residential treatment):
5. Description of organization where currently employed:
6. Likes most about present job:
7. Frustrated by:
8. Questions asked:
9. Impressions:
10. Follow-up:
    - Invite to continue process
    - Do not continue process
    - Asked to send references. Date references received:

      _____
    - Letter sent on _____ to confirm date, time, and place of next interview.
    - Letter sent on _____ to say candidate is no longer being considered for position.

willing to donate their resources. The candidate could be directed to a company that rents teleconferencing services, such as Kinko's. The organization should pay for the cost of the candidate's participation in the teleconference, which will probably be cheaper than travel and lodging expenses to bring the candidate to the office.

It is always good practice to send candidates information regarding the organization—brochures, bylaws, annual reports, and the Board's perceptions on what they expect from a new ED and what skills and character qualities the new ED should possess. In addition, the newly revised job description should be sent. An organizational chart and any other specifics about the ED's position would also be helpful. These pieces of information provide the candidate with a picture of the position and its responsibilities, and of the organization and its strengths and challenges.

The following are examples of questions that could be asked of candidates invited to participate in this first face-to-face interview.

- What was one job-related incident that disappointed you?

    Why were you disappointed?

    How did you handle the disappointment?

    How would you avoid having a repetition of this incident?

- What motivated you to seek this position with our organization?

- What do you think you will like most about being Executive Director of our organization? Why?

- What do you think will be your greatest challenge when you become our next Executive Director? Why?

- You have had an opportunity to review the Board's expectations for the next Executive Director. How would you go about meeting at least three of the Board's expectations?

Expectation One:

Expectation Two:

Expectation Three:

- The Board has identified a number of skills that will be needed by the new Executive Director. Which of those skills do you feel most comfortable with? Why?

- How would you go about guiding the organization to fulfill its vision as expressed by the Board?

Be sure to leave time for the candidates to ask questions of their own.

Exhibit 6.3 is a sample rating form that may be helpful after the first face-to-face interview. The organization may want to add other qualities that may be important to its needs, such as speaking skills, charisma, ability to relate to specific groups (such as individuals of great influence or those who are poor, individuals with disabilities, the elderly), knowledge of the accreditation process, or education and level of experience.

The Next Interview

As a result of the first face-to-face interview, only the top three or four candidates should remain in contention. At this point, the process can go in either of two directions: the candidates can be invited to meet with the Search Committee or the Board, or they can be invited to visit the organization's offices and programs. Having the candidates come to the offices of the organization lends itself to scheduling a meeting between the candidate and the key management staff and other stakeholder groups.

Reference Checks

Before the final interviews with the Search Committee or Board, it is essential to check each candidate's references. Once again it is

Exhibit 6.3.   Sample First Face-to-Face Interview Worksheet

Rating: 1 = Poor; 2 = Fair; 3 = Good; 4 = Very Good; 5 = Outstanding

Knowledge of:

    Area of Focus of Organization: _____

    Fundraising: _____

    Fiscal Management: _____

    Systems Management: _____

Ability to Communicate Effectively _____

Problem-Solving Skills _____

Administration and Management Style _____

Public Relations and Marketing _____

Attitude _____

Ability to Relate to Interviewer _____

Appearance _____

Sense of Humor _____

Overall Rating _____

Fundraising Skills _____

Should this individual be invited back for an interview with the Search
Committee or Board of Directors?

☐   Yes   Why? _____

☐   No   Why? _____

Is this candidate your:

☐   First Choice

☐   Second Choice

☐   Third Choice

☐   No Choice

imperative for the search facilitator to develop a set of questions to be used with all references. In today's litigious environment, obtaining candid information about a candidate may be difficult. Many companies and individuals do not provide any information about an employee's performance in writing or verbally. The only information you may be able to obtain is confirmation of employment, the position held, dates of employment, and salary.

In some cases, information may not be provided without a written request from the organization on its letterhead, accompanied with a release from the candidate. It is prudent to develop a "Request for Information" form for candidates to sign.

When you do contact the references, try to engage them in a casual conversation about the candidate, giving them a brief description of the organization seeking the information and the position for which the candidate is being considered. This information may offset any reluctance to share information. After the usual introductions, request permission to ask a few questions about the candidate.

If the reference is willing to respond to the questions, start with the preliminaries, such as these:

- How do you know the candidate? (As a coworker, supervisor, or supervisee?)

- How long have you known the candidate?

- What strengths does the candidate have as a leader?

- If the candidate were your employee and in your office for the annual review process, what areas of improvement would you suggest for the coming year? (The reference may be reluctant to share this type of information. It may help if the reference is reminded that "no one is perfect; knowing someone's limitations is important if one is to work to improve them or to compensate for them.")

- How did the candidate's coworkers feel about working together?

- How did the candidate relate to the organization's Board and other volunteers?

- What was the candidate's contribution to the organization?

- What challenge did the candidate have to address and how well was the issue resolved?

- Do you consider the candidate a visionary leader? Why or why not?

- Would you hire the candidate for a major leadership role in your organization? If not, why not?

Other questions that specifically relate to the organization's challenges, such as fundraising and capital campaigns, may also be included.

Be sure to thank references for their candor and assistance. Assure them that their remarks will be held in strictest confidence.

Individual Interviews with Search Committee and Board

Prior to the final interview with the Board, the search committee or search firm should compile a brief summary of each of the candidates. The summary should include information about the candidate's background, a brief review of the results of the reference checks, and a general statement about strengths and limitations. You may want to include impressions the staff and other stakeholders may have expressed after their meeting with the candidate.

The interview with the Search Committee or the full Board is similar in structure to the other interviews. Develop a series of questions for the interviews, perhaps along with a scenario like the one described earlier for the candidates to respond to. The Search

Committee or Board should take time to individually rate each candidate and then spend time discussing each candidate.

When the Search Committee is conducting the interviews, the goal is to decide which of the candidates should be invited to meet with the Board for the final interviews. When the Board is conducting the interviews, the goal is to select the next ED.

Prior to the interviews, the Board may want to send the most recent copy of the organization's strategic plan, last year's audit report, last month's financial report, and a copy of the organization's personnel policies and procedures. These documents will provide important information for the final candidates and an opportunity for the Board to ask questions regarding the candidate's impression of the organization and ideas for improving its position fiscally, programmatically, and administratively.

The following are examples of questions that could be used by either the Search Committee or Board when interviewing the final candidates.

- Briefly review your employment history and tell us a little about yourself, including:

  Present position?

  What aspects of your present job do you like?

  What aspects of your job would you change?

- What was the most innovative idea you introduced to your employers?

- How do you overcome objections to your ideas?

- Having reviewed the job description, describe how your strengths would enhance our organization.

- How would you describe the relationship between a Board and its Executive Director in a nonprofit organization?

- Why would you like to be Executive Director of our organization?

- Why should we hire you over the other candidates?

- Describe one time in your career in which you designed or implemented a new management or office system.

- What are the first five things you would do if you become Executive Director of our organization?

- What do you believe are the top four challenges facing organizations such as ours, now and in the future?

- What areas do you consider essential in supervising and overseeing the work of the management team?

- What personal and professional accomplishments are you most proud of?

- What questions do you dread most during an interview?

- What compensation, including salary and benefits, do you want to earn and can you reasonably ask for?

- What are the most important benefits, other than salary, that would prompt you to work for this organization?

- What questions do you have of us?

- If offered the position, when could you be ready to take it?

Another point to consider in choosing someone to serve as ED, particularly if the organization has serious problems that need to be cleaned up, is how long the ED plans to stay. Many EDs believe that to bring about the needed changes in organizations they have to be prepared to change jobs every three to five years. They see themselves in the position of the proverbial minister who works hard to raise the money and oversee the building of a new church. By the time the first sermon is to be given in the new church, however, this minister has been replaced. Why? Because making the tough decisions, putting pressure on the congregants to donate the money to build the new church, and dealing with the Building Committee on the color of the sanctuary left the minister with too much negative baggage to be effective, so he had to move on.

Whether one agrees with that approach, the mobility of some EDs should be calculated into the hiring process. If the Board knows that this is the candidate's career plan that fact needs to be included in the deliberations about offering the individual the job. Some situations call for retaining a new ED for a very short time to accomplish specific goals. For example, an ED who expects the job to last no more than three to five years may feel unencumbered enough to challenge agency sacred cows. It's apt to be easier for a short-timer to decide it is appropriate to initiate a major reorganization of the agency. (Remember letter #2.)

Knowing that the ED is being hired to clean up a mess in ways likely to build a cadre of antagonists should alert the Board to the fact that it may be in everyone's interest that the ED be recognized as a short-timer.

Exhibit 6.4 is a sample of the rating form that the Search Committee or the Board may want to use. The organization may want to add other qualities that may be specifically important to its needs, such as speaking skills, charisma, ability to relate to specific groups (such as individuals of great influence or those who are poor, individuals with disabilities, the elderly), knowledge of the accreditation process, education, and level of experience.

Exhibit 6.4.   Sample Final Interview Worksheet

Rating: 1 = Poor; 2 = Fair; 3 = Good; 4 = Very Good; 5 = Outstanding

Knowledge of:

    Mission _____

    Fundraising _____

    Fiscal Management _____

    Systems Management _____

Ability to Communicate Effectively _____

Problem-Solving Skills _____

Administration and Management Style _____

Public Relations and Marketing _____

Appearance _____

Attitude _____

Ability to Relate to Interviewer _____

Sense of Humor _____

Information Technology _____

Overall Rating _____

Should this individual be invited back for an interview with the organization's full Board?

☐   Yes Why? _____

☐   No Why? _____

Is this candidate your:

☐   First Choice

☐   Second Choice

☐   Third Choice

☐   No Choice

7

Negotiating, Hiring, and Orienting

After the Board has interviewed the final candidates and discussed their qualifications, it should be able to agree which candidate will get the offer. The Board should authorize its President and one other Board member to meet with the candidate to offer the position and negotiate the conditions of employment. These would include the compensation package, the starting date, the amount of relocation reimbursement if needed, the timelines of a probationary period, if one is to be initiated, the date of the first job performance evaluation, a date when a list of job performance goals will be finalized, and any other arrangements that may be needed to seal the deal.

Throughout this process, as in the earlier stages of the search, the Board may find that its own resources are insufficient to manage the transition smoothly. The latter part of this chapter discusses the use of executive transition management services, a resource that has been emerging in response to the recognized need to provide assistance to nonprofit Boards during this tense period in an organization's life.

Closing the Deal

The services of a search firm, if the organization has retained one, can still be useful during the final negotiations. A search firm can

YOU MAY WANT TO CONSIDER
A SEARCH FIRM TO HELP YOU
MOVE IN THE SAME DIRECTION

help determine a reasonable compensation package, as judged by industry standards, and can assist in the discussions and negotiations with the individual being offered the position. The firm may also be helpful in finding ways to resolve disagreements that have reached a point of impasse. Having an outsider to mediate and, if necessary, arbitrate points of contention may help resolve the issues and get the relationship off on the right footing. How the discussions and negotiations are conducted and resolved may have an immediate impact and possible long-term implications on the relationship between the Board and the new ED. Both parties must enter these discussions with an attitude of wanting them to be a win-win experience.

We have known candidates to walk away from job offers because of the way the Board handled negotiations on compensation. We have also heard of Boards' holding firm to reasonable offers when the candidate's demands become unrealistic. As noted in Chapter Six, it is always best to be sure the specifics of the candidate's compensation expectations are clear and the organization's ability to respond to those expectations is known fairly early in the process.

Many of our clients ask if the Board should offer a contract to formalize the agreement. That question has no correct answer. The deciding factor is usually the standards in the organization's industry. Various areas of the nonprofit community offer contracts to EDs as a routine way of doing business, while in other nonprofit arenas a contract would be rare. If a contract is used, an attorney should draw it up.

Whether a contract is needed or not, it may be necessary to provide the chosen ED with a letter of appointment. This may be an interim agreement between the individual and the organization before a contract is finalized or it may be all that is necessary to finalize the deal. A letter of appointment verifies the agreement between the individual and the Board and provides the new ED with the assurance that it is safe to initiate activities required before the first day on the job, such as submitting a resignation letter to the present employer. Here again, the organization's attorney should draft the letter of agreement.

Orientation

The transition is not over once the new ED assumes the job. In fact, the most important part of the ED transition process is just beginning: orientation.

The new ED should have the opportunity to conduct a series of meetings, including the following:

- Meeting with each member of the Board individually to become acquainted and discuss their individual perceptions and priorities.

- Meeting with members of the organization's management team and other members of the staff to learn more about staff morale and priority issues.

- Meeting with the primary investors in the organization, which include public and private funders.

- Meeting with a representative group of individuals who receive services from the organization.

- Meeting with Finance Committee, auditors, and the Business Department to become acquainted with the organization's financial operations, management, and challenges.

- Meeting with the Board's Personnel Committee to become acquainted with personnel policies and procedures.

Eventually the new ED will want to reach outside the organization and meet with leaders of other organizations providing services to the same and different consumer groups. It will also be necessary to meet with public policymakers at the local, state, and national level, and with the community's corporate and philanthropic leaders.

The Board, the new ED, and other key management staff may want to participate in a retreat that focuses on discussing issues of shared leadership and the roles and responsibilities of the Board and ED. The assistance of a skilled facilitator is apt to be useful for this session.

The Board and ED need to develop specific, measurable job performance milestones for both parties for the first six months. This process should be repeated every six to twelve months.

The Board's commitment to the professional development of the new ED can be demonstrated when developing a plan that would include attendance at state, regional, national, or even international conferences relevant to the organization's vision and mission. The plan may include participation in nonprofit management and leadership enhancement seminars, and in the courses available at a number of universities. Part of the plan may include a commitment from the ED to prepare a presentation on key points for the Board and the agency's staff upon returning from a conference or seminar.

The Board and ED should agree on a target date to begin revisiting the agency's mission, vision, and strategic plan. The new ED must have an imprint on that plan, and the process should begin within the first three to six months after the ED has been hired.

Last, but certainly not least, the Board and ED need to discuss and agree on how they will maintain an open and honest relationship through communication. Weekly meetings with the Board leadership is always a good plan. Periodic phone calls from any member of the Board are always appreciated by a beginning or seasoned ED. Both parties understand the importance of the concepts of *no surprises*—and *full disclosure*.

Using Executive Transition Management Services

Executive transition management services (TMS) are available through many nonprofit support organizations and a few specialized independent consultants. These organizations and consultants have developed expertise and resources in the following array of services:

- *Organizational analysis and change planning:* The TMS can conduct an independent, objective management and operational evaluation of the organization and provide the Board with a comprehensive report that includes a plan of correction for problem areas.

- *Planning a transition process:* With its expertise, the TMS provider can quickly assess the organization's transition needs and then provide the nonprofit Board with a well-coordinated and well-planned transition process.

- *Interim ED placement and management:* Most TMS organizations have cultivated a cadre of highly qualified individuals who are available to provide interim ED services. The TMS provider should be able to suggest two or three candidates for the interim ED's position for consideration by the Board or Search Committee. The candidates presented will possess the expertise and experience needed to successfully perform the specific responsibilities of the position.

Most TMS providers will offer some form of support to the Board and interim ED during the placement period. This gives the nonprofit Board assurance that in the event of any problems with the interim ED or any unexpected internal or external issues there is a reliable resource that can be called upon for assistance.

Planning and Implementing the Comprehensive Executive Search Process

Many TMS providers are available to assist the nonprofit Board in planning and implementing a comprehensive executive search process. Part of that service will include assisting the Board in identifying the organization's present strengths, problems, opportunities, and threats. The TMS will be able to facilitate the review, developing a five- or ten-year vision statement. The resulting vision statement, along with the identification of the Board's expectations of the new ED, will facilitate the direction of the executive search process.

The TMS may also work with a Search Committee or Board to recruit, screen, and hire a permanent ED. It will also help the Board develop a plan to orient and retain that executive. Some transition management services provide ongoing support to the Board and the new ED to assist them through the first year.

Succession Planning

The TMS is also available to provide guidance to the nonprofit Board in planning and implementing an agencywide system of leadership enhancement and succession planning that not only addresses the ED's position but all management and supervisory positions. Succession planning should be an agencywide commitment.

The efficacy of TMS has been demonstrated by a number of projects that focus on this long-neglected area of nonprofit management. The Neighborhood Reinvestment Corporation studied the impact of executive transition on forty nonprofits. Ten organizations were provided the assistance of a TMS, and reported an increase in the length of tenure with the new ED and also an increase in the level of successful completion of organizational goals.

When the Board avails itself of services and expertise of organizations or consultants who specialize in TMS, it assures that the results of the appointment of an interim ED and the preparation and implementation of the executive search will be successful. The services available from TMS providers may vary, so be sure to ask what they offer your nonprofit community.

Helpful Sources

Providers of TMS may be located through the following resources:

- The local United Way

- The state's nonprofit management organization (www.ncna.org)

- A local university or college that has a nonprofit management program

- BoardSource (formerly the National Center for Nonprofit Boards) (www.boardsource.org)

- The Alliance for Nonprofit Management (www.allianceonline.org)

- The Association of Fundraising Professionals (www.nsfre.org)

- American Society of Association Executives (www.asaenet.org)

Questions to Ask a Transition Management Service Provider

The committee should request a list of services provided by the TMS as well as a list of past clients and at least three references. The following is a list of questions you may want to ask the TMS provider.

- What are the fees for your services?

- What services do the fees include?

- Are travel, meals, lodging, mailings, long-distance calls, or other related out-of-pocket expenses included?

- If not, what are the projected costs for expenses? (Be sure to agree that receipts will accompany all invoices for out-of-pocket expenses or establish a per diem rate.)

- Will adjustments to fees be possible if the TMS provider is retained for more than one service, such as providing interim ED services and conducting the search for the new ED?

- How soon can it make a placement for the interim ED's position?

- What is the role of the organization's Board in selecting the interim ED?

- Is the interim an employee of the TMS provider or an independent contractor?

- Who hires and fires the interim ED, the Board or the provider of TMS?

- Who supervises the interim ED?

- How long will the interim ED be committed to stay?

- What happens if the interim ED leaves the position before the agreed-upon time? Will the provider of TMS assume responsibility for a replacement? Will there be an additional fee for that service?

- How many hours per week will the interim ED commit to? (Sixteen, twenty-four, forty or more. . . .)

- What process do you use to conduct the executive search? What is the role of the Board and its Search Committee?

- Is there a guarantee provided in case the newly hired ED does not stay with the organization for at least a year?

- What supports are provided to the Board and the new ED during the first year? Is there a charge for this service?

8

The Ingredients of a Successful Board–Executive Director Relationship

The new ED will come to the organization with a high level of excitement, enthusiasm, commitment, and dedication—and expectations that the Board will be trusting, supportive, responsive, and encouraging. Many have referred to this time as a "honeymoon period." Yet this is not the time for the Board to abdicate its responsibility as the governing body of the organization. Both Board and ED must have a clear understanding of each other's roles and responsibilities in the critical first six months to a year. Developing that understanding may require the assistance of an outside consultant to facilitate the discussions and bring both to a consensus. Reviewing this understanding periodically may be necessary as circumstances change with time.

The important factor to keep in mind is that change at the executive level provides the Board and organization the opportunity for renewal and revitalization. To ignore opportunity may result in the new ED's leaving within the first one or two years. The loss of an ED every few years often indicates internal problems that may well start with the way the relationship between the ED and Board functions.

Earlier in this book, we identified the seven factors that influence an ED's leaving. Only one of those factors cannot be prevented, the Sudden Loss Factor. It is the responsibility of the Board to ensure that skilled and successful EDs stay with the organization.

ANNUAL EXECUTIVE EVALUATION
CAN REDUCE SURPRISES

As the new ED steps into the job, the Board should be thinking about how to hold on to the officer it worked so hard to find. A good start is to foster trust and respect.

We believe that a successful Board–ED relationship is based on ingredients that must blend together as smoothly and securely as a good lunch. A foundation of trust and respect is like the plate the food is on. It provides stability and strength to the presentation. The other ingredients can be compared to a sandwich. The one we have in mind contains no bologna, nor is it unstable like the fabled Dagwood sandwich.

Fostering a relationship of trust and respect between an Executive Director and a Board is one of the keys to holding on to a good ED. It also bodes well for a smooth transition when the time does come for the Executive Director to leave.

Trust and respect are two-way streets, and both must be earned. Respecting and trusting someone does not necessarily mean agreeing with everything that person says. Agreeing to disagree and still maintaining a respectful and trusting relationship demonstrates the maturity of the relationship.

Because the Board and the ED share the leadership of the organization, their relationship is often characterized as one of dynamic tension. That shared responsibility makes it even more important that each trusts and respects the other's roles. When the Board or ED crosses into the other's purview of leadership, it usually indicates that trust and respect have declined or are absent altogether. If the balance of leadership is skewed one way or another, the organization is out of sync with what is considered a standard management profile for nonprofit organizations. In other words, the plate is cracked and no longer provides the stability to support the relationship.

Interactions between the Board and the ED are inherently complicated because of the employer-employee relationship that exists between the parties. Building a trusting and respectful relationship between the two partners helps transcend the employer-employee dynamic. Either or both parties may face challenges to this fragile relationship.

That is why it is so important to know how to build a healthy (no-bologna) relationship between the Board and ED.

The Seven C's

The foundation of trust and respect is enhanced with a relationship that contains seven ingredients. (As you can see, we are still fond of the number seven.) These are our Seven C's (not to be confused with the Seven Seas of Sinbad the Sailor fame or the salad dressing):

- Communication

- Collaboration

- Compatibility

- Consensus

- Compromise

- Candor

- Communication

The blending of these seven C's creates a strong, nurturing, and satisfying no-bologna relationship, which must be maintained and enhanced with the commitment and work of both Board and ED.

Communication (Twice)

Communication is listed twice (no, we did not make a mistake) because it is the first and the last most important component for establishing and maintaining a meaningful and successful relationship. It is also first and last because communication goes both ways in the Board and ED relationship. Communication is an all-encompassing and essential element if the other five C's are to be successfully implemented. If well-defined lines of communication are not established, chaos is a certainty.

The card game Bridge is based on two partners communicating with each other through a series of bids. Forming a "bridge" of information allows the partners to reach a decision to be on the offense and attempt to score points or go on the defense and prevent the opponents from making points. If they are successful in bridging the communication gap, they may be able to score enough points to win the game.

Good communication between the Board and ED is a matter of sharing information and points of view, which enhances their *shared leadership*. The Board and ED have a joint responsibility to build a solid communication bridge. Just as there are rules for communication in the game of Bridge, there are structures that a Board President and an Executive Director can follow to increase the chances of forming a winning alliance.

When Carol was a Board President, the ED took her out to dinner to talk about ground rules for how they could best communicate. The ED asked Carol when and how she would like to work together. They decided to have an in-person meeting every other week and by phone on Friday afternoons the alternate weeks. Carol asked that the ED not call after 9:30 P.M. unless it was an emergency, although 5:30 A.M. was fine, because her family were early risers. The ED asked Carol to put "important" on the subject line of any e-mail message that really had to get through, because he received over a hundred a day and didn't want anything that mattered to get lost.

They also discussed how they were going to work on the agenda, where they would sit in Board meetings, and how the ED's secretary kept his schedule. They were able to begin working together effectively from the beginning because of these important pieces of communication.

Another example: Imagine the chagrin, not to mention anger, when the Board President said to the United Way Site Committee, "We have seven programs to prevent and treat domestic violence."

A committee member said, "I count eight programs." The ED had started a program without getting agreement or even notifying the Board. Within a month, the Board President and many of his friends had left the Board. They took their expertise with them, and the organization missed out on a major chunk of corporate and personal dollars they would have brought in.

In marketing, the operative word is repetition, repetition, repetition. In real estate it is location, location, location. In relationship building it is *communication, communication, communication*.

Collaboration

Collaboration should be the primary methodology for the Board and ED to facilitate their partnership. Lack of collaborating on decision making is a critical sign that the partnership is in trouble. Both Board and ED must be committed to ensuring that the principle of working together and sharing ideas is a basic core value on both sides and therefore should be applied to the entire organization's operations and governance. Without collaboration the Board and ED may find themselves working at odds with each other.

A classic example comes in the area of fundraising—whether the ED is the development professional or simply the point person between the Board and the development staff. If the Board and ED are not working in concert with each other in a collaborative way, a Board member may wind up asking a corporation or individual for $2,000 when the Development Director has been working on a $100,000 proposal. The Board member looks foolish, the organization's reputation suffers, and there is a good chance that the group will find itself with a $2,000 check rather than a $100,000 donation!

Compatibility

Compatibility—the sheer ability to get along with each other comfortably—is an important component to the success of any relationship. The Board and the ED should be compatible in their vision and mission for the organization. Both must be committed to adhering to and fostering the core values of the organization. If either partner deviates from these foundations of good governance, then the compatibility with the organization and with the other partner needs to be addressed and resolved as quickly as possible. The formation of the Board and ED into a compatible team is analogous to the blending of compatible ingredients in a sandwich. Mayonnaise and jelly are not compatible, but peanut butter and jelly are; they make the ultimate compatible sandwich.

When we conduct executive searches, we often tell our clients that the final two or three candidates will have all the experiences and skill sets needed to meet and exceed the Board's expectations. The candidates should also be compatible with the vision, mission, and values of the organization. The real test will be if the candidates are compatible with the Board. Is the chemistry there? Do the bells ring and the whistles blow during the interview with the candidate?

Given a good search process, the ED and Board should be compatible from the start. But over time, that compatibility can deteriorate. Remember the seventh factor why EDs leave an organization, the Ten-Year Factor? Often by that time, the Board and the ED no longer have a fit. The chemistry is gone. When that happens, it is usually time for the ED to move on.

The compatibility factor is, of course, based on the premise that the Board and ED trust and respect each other. Without those two dynamics, compatibility is impossible.

Consensus

Consensus building is a very important part of group dynamics, because it involves the give-and-take of decision making. Coming to consensus means parties must communicate, respect, and trust each other's opinions, and consider ways to bring all ideas together into one mutually acceptable decision. Our formula for reaching consensus involves three factors:

- All parties have had an equal opportunity to express opinions.

- At least 80 percent of the group agree with the final decision.

- Everyone leaves the discussion agreeing to support the final decision.

When everything works as it should, this type of consensus is the essence of a well-functioning relationship and decision-making process.

The Board of the Delta Center for Independent Living in St. Charles, Missouri, provides an excellent example. An extremely difficult issue arose: Should the Delta Center for Independent Living permit clients to hire attendants who had failed a police background check? Board members had very strong feelings. The disabled Board members who used attendants believed that the consumer should make the decision. The nondisabled Board members believed that the consumer and the Center should be protected. A facilitator was hired to help the decision making in the Board meeting, partially because the president wanted to be free to comment and didn't want to be responsible for leading the meeting at the same time. Discussions were frank, impassioned, but always respectful. The Board came to a compromise solution barring attendants who had been convicted of violent crimes. It took two long, hard meetings to come to consensus, but the Board felt that it had been involved in an important process that would set a strategic guideline for the agency to better serve its clients.

The opposite of the consensus-building process is dictatorial decision making. When unilateral decisions are made outside the acceptable roles and responsibilities, the partnership no longer exists. The Board and ED must work to keep this from happening.

Compromise

Compromise is the essence of any relationship. Finding ways to come together to make a decision that results in consensus requires the ability to compromise. Both the Board and ED have to be committed to finding ways to have a win–win solution to a debate. Neither party should be closed to the other's opinion, nor should they be so entrenched in their own positions that movement to the middle is impossible. The ability to compromise is a sign of maturity and security.

The art of compromise may be most important when it comes to the negotiations regarding the organization's budget. The ED may feel strongly that money should be allocated in one direction, while the Board and its Finance Committee may think that direction is wrong or that there aren't enough resources to meet the ED's requests. Finding a way to satisfy the ED's commitment to a specific area of the budget and yet not jeopardize the Board's fiduciary responsibilities is important. Always look for ways for both the Board and the Executive Director to feel they have at least achieved their goal to some degree. As the old saying goes, having half an apple now is better than not having any apple—or waiting for a whole apple later, which may never come.

Candor

Candor is the seventh ingredient to the no-bologna sandwich of Board-staff relations. The ability to be open and honest with each other is vital to the communication process. Expressing what is on your mind and feeling that the person listening is receptive to your comments is a process that enhances the relationship. It fosters a level of confidence that permits debate within the atmosphere of respect for each other's opinions.

Without candor, issues of concern may turn into problems, and problems may grow into crisis. It is always best to address issues when they are just at the concern stage. That way the issue has not reached such an emotional intensity that other opinions may not be heard. If the concern is not resolved quickly through compromise and consensus building, finding resolution to a problem or crisis will be proportionally more difficult as the intensity of emotions rises.

Both Board and ED must agree that they will come to each other and express how they feel at the time. They must agree not to let issues fester until they become problems or a crisis.

Whenever Dick assumes an interim position with an organization, he establishes some basic understandings with both Board and staff. One of those principles of conduct is that he cannot solve problems without knowing that they exist. Therefore, he asks the Board and staff to pledge to come to him with any concern they may have before it gets out of hand and requires a larger amount of time to find a reasonable solution.

Tools and Techniques for Encouraging and Strengthening the Seven C's

The Board and the ED each have a role in reinforcing the seven C's, but the Board has responsibility for establishing systems to keep the relationship humming and to resolve problems as they arise. To do that, the Board should take the following steps:

- Establish a built-in process for evaluating the ED's job performance, which should include an ongoing dialogue between the two partners. Setting specific goals will aid the ED and Board when the annual job performance review is conducted. It is important that the ED and Board agree to the priorities and expectations.

- Have an ongoing process for conducting a self-evaluation of how the Board is operating. The Board should seek the ED's opinions and perceptions and give them strong consideration.

- Establish a method of sharing concerns, whether it is one-on-one between the ED and Board President or a conversation between the ED and the Executive Committee. Whatever the approach, either party— the Board or the Executive Director—should be free to implement it as soon as concerns begin to inhibit the relationship.

- Hire an outside independent consultant or arbitrator to facilitate the discussion, if necessary. Either the Board or the ED could take this step. (It's like marriage counseling: Either the husband or the wife can make the call.) In either case, finding such an outside consultant must be done carefully to make sure that the individual is a skilled arbitrator and facilitator.

These systems and procedures can go a long way toward keeping a relationship strong and nipping concerns before they explode into full-blown crises.

In summation, the seven C's—communication, collaboration, compatibility, consensus, compromise, candor and communication again—are necessary ingredients to a no-bologna Board-staff relationship. The Board-staff relationship must be served on a plate of trust and respect. It takes work time and commitment for the sandwich to come together and become palatable for all at the table. Without them, however, your organization may not be able to successfully fulfill its mission.

As Henry Ford once said, "Coming together is the beginning, staying together is progress, and working together is success."

The following poem exemplifies the responsibility of the Board and ED for ensuring an effective transfer of leadership.

The Bridge Builder

An old man, going a lone highway,
Came at the evening, cold and gray,
To a chasm, vast and deep and wide,
Through which was flowing a sullen tide.
The old man crossed in the twilight dim—
That sullen stream had no fears for him;
But he turned, when he reached the other side,

And built a bridge to span the tide.
"Old man," said a fellow pilgrim near,
"You are wasting strength in building here,
Your journey will end with the ending day;
You never again must pass this way.
You have crossed the chasm, deep and wide,
Why build you the bridge at the eventide?"
The builder lifted his old gray head.
"Good friend, in the path I have come," he said,
"There followeth after me today
A youth whose feet must pass this way.
This chasm that has been naught to me
To that fair-haired youth may a pitfall be.
He, too, must cross in the twilight dim;
Good friend, I am building the bridge for him."

Will Allen Dromgoole

Guidelines for ED Candidates

Throughout this book we have focused on what the Board and its representatives should be doing as part of the transition process. This section is designed to assist candidates for the ED's position by providing guidelines and suggested questions that may be useful in the search and the negotiations.

- Before you answer an announcement that a position is available, be sure you have the qualifications and experience to be considered by the organization.

- When contacted by the organization, be prepared to answer questions about your experience and qualifications. Respond with confidence and be concise but thorough.

- Do not make disparaging remarks about supervisors, Boards, or organizations you have worked with in the past.

- Provide references that will provide information about your expertise and skills as a leader and motivator.

The following are questions that may help you assess the position and the organization.

- How long has the present ED been with the organization?

- Why is the present ED leaving?

- When will the present ED be leaving?

- Will there be any overlap with the departing ED? If so, how long?

- Is someone filling the role of interim ED? Who?

- Is the interim ED a candidate for the permanent position?

- What is the process being used to select the next ED?

- What are the Board's expectations for the next ED?

- Where does the Board want the organization to be in the next five to ten years?

- What are the three most critical issues facing the organization?

- Are there any pending EEOC complaints against the organization?

- Are there any liens or litigation pending against the organization?

- When does the Board Presidency change hands?

- Will the new ED be offered a contract?

- Are there opportunities to attend conferences and seminars related to the position?

Before committing to meet with the Search Committee or Board in the final phase of the process, the candidate and the Board should discuss who will pay for travel, lodging, and food expenses associated with the final interview. Some organizations may cover such costs. It does not hurt to ask. The candidate should request a packet of information on the organization if one isn't offered up front. The packet should include the following:

- Job description for the ED's position.

- List of expectations and skill sets as described by the present Board.

- An organizational chart.

- A list of services and programs provided by the organization.

- The organization's bylaws.

- The most recent copy of the organization's strategic plan, which should include vision, mission, and values statement, strategic goals and objectives, and action steps for each objective.

- Copies of the last three annual audits, including a copy of the management letter. If an audit is not available, find out why. Perhaps the organization is too small or too new to have needed one.

- The most recent financial statement.

- The organization's personnel policies and procedures.

A candidate for an ED position should try to obtain as much information as possible about the organization and the community it serves prior to participating in the interview process.

Resource A

Example of an Executive Search Agreement

This Agreement made and entered into this ___ day of _____ by and between _____ [name of executive search company] _____ [hereinafter called "the company"] and the _____ [name of organization] _____ [hereinafter called "the organization"], for an initial period of _____ days commencing on the acceptance of this agreement. The agreement shall terminate on _____ day of _____ unless extended by written agreement by both parties.

Witnesseth:

Whereas, the company engages in the business of contracting with nonprofit organizations to provide executive search and other executive transition management services including interim Executive Director services; and

Whereas, the organization needs to find a qualified individual to be its next Executive Director,

Now, therefore, for and in consideration of the mutual covenants, promises, and payments as hereinafter set forth, the company and the organization agree as follows:

1. The organization agrees to retain the company for the purpose of conducting an executive search as described in the company's proposal dated _____, the contents of which shall be considered part of this agreement.

138 LOSING YOUR EXECUTIVE DIRECTOR WITHOUT LOSING YOUR WAY

2. The company shall be responsible for providing no less than three final qualified candidates who meet all of the requirements provided by the organization (level of experience, expertise, compensation expectations, and the like) to the organization's Board and Search Committee for its final selection.

3. The organization shall be responsible for negotiating with the selected candidate, in good faith, the final compensation and hiring package within the previously stated parameters.

4. The organization agrees to pay the company a fee of $_____. This fee shall be paid based on the following timetable:

   a. One-third of the fee ($_____) upon the approval of this agreement.

   b. One-third of the fee ($_____) at the time the final candidates are scheduled to be interviewed by the organization's Board of Directors.

   c. The final one-third of the fee ($_____) within ten days after the new Executive Director has reported to work.

5. The organization agrees that it shall respond in a reasonable and timely manner to the company's requests for information, meeting times, and decisions. The organization shall not deliberately delay a hiring within the _____ time limit per this agreement.

6. The organization understands that the company will spend substantial investment in time and effort attempting to fulfill the executive search contract within the allocated time. Therefore, the organization understands and agrees that if it does not hire any of those final candidates presented by the company to the organization for consideration for the Executive Director's position, it may not hire any of those individuals as either Executive Director or interim Executive Director, on a full- or part-time basis, within twelve months of their being introduced to the Board by the company. If the organization should hire said candidate, it shall pay to the company a sum equal to 100 percent of the company's fee for conducting the executive search, as defined in this agreement, which sum shall be a finder's fee. The parties agree that the one (1) year re-

striction herein is reasonable, based upon the substantial time and effort expended by the company in obtaining the final candidate. If there is a disagreement regarding this matter, both parties agree to submit said claims to binding arbitration.

7. The organization agrees to reimburse the company for all out-of-pocket expenses incurred as part of the executive search process. The company will provide a detailed invoice to the organization on the first of each month. The organization will pay the company within ten days of receipt of the invoice. The company reserves the right to charge 1.5 percent carrying charge on all balances due over thirty days.

8. The company agrees to provide a guarantee pertaining to the successful hiring of the new Executive Director. The terms of the guarantee are attached to this agreement [see Resource B] and are considered part of this agreement.

9. This agreement may be amended only by a written instrument signed by both parties hereto.

10. This agreement shall be interpreted under the laws of the State of _____.

11. The parties agree that this Agreement contains all convents, promises, or other inducements made between the parties.

[Name of Company]   [Name of Organization]

By: _____   By: _____

Date: _____   Date: _____

Resource B

Example of an Executive Search Guarantee

The _____ [name of executive search company] _____ (hereafter referred to as the company) is confident that the candidates it refers to the Board of Directors of the _____ [name of organization] _____ (hereafter referred to as the organization) for consideration for the position of Executive Director will represent some of the best-qualified individuals to be found per the criteria established by the organization. The company also understands that the first year of employment is a time of transition and adjustment and that the new hire may prove unsuccessful despite the company's confidence in the individual's probable success. If either the organization or the new Executive Director decides to terminate the relationship for job-related reasons, the company will provide the following guarantee:

1. Within the first six months, if the person hired for the position has not satisfactorily demonstrated the ability to perform the duties and responsibilities as delineated in the job description and the organization decides to terminate, the company will initiate a new search process at no additional fee to the organization. Out-of-pocket expenses associated with the renewed process will be the responsibility of the organization.

2. Within the first six months, if the person hired finds that the position is not what was expected and decides to terminate employment with the organization, the company will initiate a new search

process at no additional fee to the organization. Out-of-pocket expenses associated with the renewed process will be the responsibility of the organization.

3. Within the seventh through twelfth months, if the person hired for the position has not satisfactorily demonstrated the ability to perform the duties and responsibilities as delineated in the job description and the organization decides to terminate, the company will initiate a new search process at one-half the original fee. Out-of-pocket expenses associated with the renewed process will be the responsibility of the organization.

4. Within the seventh through twelfth months, if the person hired finds that the position is not what was expected and decides to terminate employment with the organization, the company will initiate a new search process at one-half the original fee. Out-of-pocket expenses associated with the renewed process will be the responsibility of the organization.

5. The company will provide these guarantees for the first person hired by the organization.

Conditions of the Guarantee

The promised guarantee is based on the following conditions:

1. The company will conduct a survey with the members of the organization's Board of Directors to solicit their perceptions of the expertise and expectations they have for their next Executive Director. This information will be compared to the existing job description. The company will make recommended revisions to the job description based on the results of the profile developed from information provided by the organization.

2. The company will be given permission to talk to the previous Executive Director, if appropriate and available, to determine why that individual left the position.

3. The company's recommendation will be considered when the Search Committee and the Board of Directors are deciding which of the candidates to hire.

4. The company will be notified by the organization's Board President or the new Executive Director at the first indication that a problem or concern exists. The new Executive Director and representatives from the organization will meet with a representative from the company to determine the problems and concerns and develop strategies for addressing them.

5. The company will have the cooperation of the Board members in reviewing why the first process did not work.

6. This guarantee does not cover the situation if the new Executive Director voluntarily leaves the position for any unforeseen personal or family reasons (for example, death or terminal illness of the individual or an immediate family member, relocation of spouse or significant other, or any other such event).

Agreed to by:

By: _____   *[Name of Representative*
                               of the Company]

Date: _____

By: _____   *[Name of Representative*
                               of the Organization]

Date: _____

References and Other Resources

Adams, T. "Executive Transitions: How Boards and Executives Create Their Futures" *Nonprofit World,* 1998, *16*(2), 48–52.

Adams, T. "Passing the Torch: Don't Get Burned By Executive Transitions." *Neighbor Works Journal,* 1999, *17*(2), 4–7.

Albrecht, K. *The Only Thing That Matters: Brining the Power of the Customer into the Center of Your Business.* New York: Harper Business, 1992.

Bailey, S. "Executive Transitions: A Powerful Opportunity for Change": An Interview with Jan Masaoka, Executive Director of the Support Center of Nonprofit Management, July 1997. Available online: http://www.genie.org/op_opinion_001.htm. Access date: Nov. 12, 2003.

Carey, D. C., and Ogden, D. *CEO Succession.* New York: Oxford University Press, 2000.

Dambach, C., Tessier, O., and Weisman, C. *The Business Professional's Guide to Nonprofit Board Service.* Washington, D.C.: BoardSource, 2002.

Gilmore, T. N. *Making a Leadership Change: How Organizations and Leaders Can Handle Leadership Transition Successfully.* San Francisco: Jossey-Bass, 1988.

Hesselbein, F. "The Challenge of Leadership Transition." *Leader to Leader,* 1997, 6, 7.

Managing Executive Transitions: A Handbook for Nonprofit Organizations. Washington, D.C.: Neighborhood Reinvestment Corporation, Community Development Leadership Project, 1999. Available online: http://www.nw.org/. Access date: Nov. 12, 2003.

McLaughlin, T. A. *Nonprofit Mergers and Alliances: A Strategic Planning Guide.* New York: Wiley, 1998.

National Center for Nonprofit Boards. *The Nonprofit Governance Index.* Washington, D.C.: National Center for Nonprofit Boards, 2000.

Pritchett, P. *Culture Shift: The Employee Handbook for Changing Corporate Culture*. Dallas, Tex.: Pritchett and Associates, 1993.

Sage, D., and Burrello, L. *Leadership in Educational Reform: an Administrator's Guide to the Changes in Special Education*. Baltimore: Brookes, 1994.

Smith, T. S., and Goldstein, M. H. *Theory and Practice of Transition Management*. Golden, Colo.: Full Circle Consulting, 2001.

Stevens Group. *Illinois Nonprofits: Building Capacity for the Next Century*. Chicago: Illinois Facilities Fund and Donors Forum of Chicago, 1998.

Weisman, C. *A Corporate Employee's Guide to Nonprofit Board Service*. Washington, D.C.: The National Center for Nonprofit Boards, 1996.

Weisman, C. *Build a Better Board in Thirty Days: A Practical Guide for Busy Trustees*. St. Louis, Mo.: F. E. Robbins and Sons Press, 1998.

Weisman, C. *Tips on Successful Major Donor Solicitation*. St. Louis, Mo.: F. E. Robbins and Sons Press, 2002.

Weisman, C. *Secrets of Successful Boards: The Best from the Nonprofit Pros*. St. Louis, Mo.: F. E. Robbins and Sons Press, 2003.

Weisman, C. *Secrets of Successful Fundraising: The Best from the Nonprofit Pros*. St. Louis, Mo.: F. E. Robbins and Sons Press, 2003.

Weisman, C. *Secrets of Successful Retreats: The Best from the Nonprofit Pros*. St. Louis, Mo.: F. E. Robbins and Sons Press, 2003.

Wolfred, T., Allison, M., and Masaoka, J. *Leadership Lost: A Study on Executive Director Tenure and Experience*. San Francisco: Support Center for Nonprofit Management, 1999.

Index